THE SPORT OF QUEENS

Also by Dick Francis
in Pan Books

For Kicks
Odds Against
Flying Finish
Blood Sport
Forfeit
Enquiry
Rat Race
Bone Crack
Smokescreen
Slay-Ride
Knock Down
Dead Cert
Nerve
High Stakes
In the Frame
Risk
Trial Run
Whip Hand
Reflex
Twice Shy
Banker

the autobiography of

Dick Francis

The Sport of Queens

revised
Pan Books London and Sydney

First published in Great Britain 1957
by Michael Joseph Ltd
This revised edition published 1974 by
Pan Books Ltd, Cavaye Place, London SW10 9PG
9 8
© Dick Francis 1957, 1974
ISBN 0 330 26685 3
Printed and bound in Great Britain by
Hazell Watson & Viney Limited,
Member of the BPCC Group,
Aylesbury, Bucks

for
Merrick and Felix
my sons

Acknowledgements

I wish to acknowledge my sincere and permanent gratitude . . .

To Her Majesty Queen Elizabeth the Queen Mother, for the great honour of her patronage, and for her gracious consent to the title of this book.

To the Most Hon the Marquess of Abergavenny, whose generous help and constant good advice I have deeply appreciated.

To all owners and trainers who have employed me, for the fun I have had on their horses, and to my fellow jockeys for the pleasure I have found in their company.

To my neighbour, Geoffrey Boumphrey, author and inventor, for the lessons I learned from his lucid prose style.

And to Mary, my wife, for more than she will allow me to say.

Contents

ONE	Colt on a Donkey	13
TWO	Rings and Wings	29
THREE	Under Starter's Orders	44
FOUR	Black, Gold Sleeves, Red Cap	62
FIVE	It's an Up and Down Life	77
SIX	Riders and Routine	95
SEVEN	Horses	113
EIGHT	Courses	124
NINE	Chase Me a Steeple	143
TEN	The Good Years	163
ELEVEN	America	180
TWELVE	Devon Loch, 1956	190
THIRTEEN	Afterwards, 1956–1981	206
	Index	221

List of Illustrations

between pages 112 and 113

The author, aged thirteen

Dick Francis receiving the Champion Hunter rosette, 1938

Fighting Line falling at Sandown Park

Amyclas at Birmingham, 1949

Possible jumping the last fence at Aintree, 1950

Roimond jumping Becher's Brook, 1950

Silver Fame at Cheltenham, 1950

Lochroe winning at Hurst Park, 1954

Devon Loch in the Blindley Heath Handicap, 1955

In the parade ring before the 1956 Grand National

M'as-Tu-Vu at Lingfield, 1956

Dick Francis in his paddock, 1972

Devon Loch rose to the last fence confidently, and landed cleanly. Behind him lay more than four miles and the thirty fences of the Grand National Steeplechase, and in front, only a few hundred yards stretched to the winning post.

In all my life I have never experienced a greater joy than the knowledge that I was about to win the National.

As we drew away from E.S.B. the cheers of the crowds greeting Her Majesty Queen Elizabeth the Queen Mother's great horse seemed to echo my own exhilaration. I had no anxieties. Devon Loch was galloping fast, incredibly fresh after the long race, and I had only to keep him going collectedly in the easy rhythm he had established.

The winning post drew rapidly nearer, the cheers were coming to a buffeting crescendo, and I was rejoicing that I was being a partner in fulfilling the dream of the horse's Royal owner. There were less than fifty yards of flat green grass to cover, and in about ten more strides we would have been home.

The calamity which overtook us was sudden, terrible, and completely without warning to either the horse or me. In one stride he was bounding smoothly along, a poem of controlled motion; in the next, his hind legs stiffened and refused to function. He fell flat on his belly, his limbs splayed out sideways and backwards in unnatural angles, and when he stood up he could hardly move.

Even then, if he could have got going again he might still have had a chance, because we had been a long way clear of E.S.B. : but the rhythm was shattered, the dream was over, and the race was lost.

Every steeplechase jockey has two ambitions. One is to ride more winners than anyone else in one season, and become Champion Jockey for that year. The other is to win the Grand National at Aintree. This is the story of how with great good fortune I achieved the first, and came so heartbreakingly close to the second.

ONE

Colt on a Donkey

I learned to ride when I was five, on a donkey.

I rode without a saddle, partly because it was a pet theory of my father's that riding bareback was the best way to learn balance, but mostly because there was, anyway, no saddle to fit her high bony back.

As soon as he saw me urging this long-suffering animal with more enthusiasm than style over a very small rail fence, my elder brother offered me the princely sum of sixpence if I could jump the fence sitting backwards. At that time I was saving all my pocket money to buy a toy farm, so this offer could not be ignored. I turned round awkwardly with my knees pressed hard into her flanks, pointed the donkey's head at the fence, and kicked.

The donkey started off, and I went head first over her tail.

When my brother could control his mirth at this event he collected the moke, who was fortunately too lazy to run away, and returned me to her back. We went through this programme twice more, and it became obvious that my brother's laughter was beginning to cause him considerable pain.

However, after a pause, during which I rubbed the parts of me which had hit the ground, and my brother rubbed his stomach, gasped for breath, and wiped the tears from his cheeks, we tried again.

He thought his sixpence was quite safe, but I wanted my farm very much.

This time I stayed on until the donkey jumped, but we landed on opposite sides of the fence.

Finally, with my nine-year-old brother shouting and

chasing us with a waving stick, the donkey and I jumped the fence together, landed together, and came precariously to a halt.

The sixpence was solemnly handed over, and in this way I earned my first riding fee. In my heart, from that moment, I became a professional horseman.

The donkey was our constant holiday companion. She lived a peaceful existence for nine months of the year on my grandfather's farm in Pembrokeshire, but during every Easter and summer school holidays, and occasionally at Christmas too, she was stirred to reluctant activity by two pitiless small boys. Often, when we had managed to borrow a neighbouring donkey as well, we went on long and roundabout journeys, meeting hair-raising and imaginary adventures on the way.

The fields of Coedcanlas, my grandfather's farm, sloped down to the Cleddeau estuary, and rose and fell over the surrounding hills, so that we had a large and exciting terrain for our explorations, and could get comfortably beyond the range of even the loudest grown-up voice calling us in at bedtime.

On other days we harnessed the donkeys into donkey-carts, and staged spectacular chariot races of several laps around a small rough field. With fearsome yells and much carrot-dangling we managed to make the donkeys break into a slow trot, but by the end of each half-mile event they were hardly out of breath, while we were quite spent from our exertions.

We loved the farm. It was our mother's home, and I was born there.

The farmhouse was large, creeper-grown, and white-washed, with solid buttressy walls six feet thick. I used to lie full length on my stomach on the window seats in the deep embrasures, looking out of the window, with my feet to the middle of the room. The house was sunk into the ground, so that one had to go down into the hall, and there was a short outside staircase which led directly, through a trellised archway covered with wistaria, to the bedrooms on the first floor.

Mercifully much older than the hideous architecture which has been disfiguring the Welsh landscape for the last hundred and fifty years, it folded gently into its surroundings, instead of glaring from them aggressively in orange brick.

Willie Thomas was a great man in the Victorian tradition. He ruled his children with a firm hand, even after they had grown up and married, and his idea of a good upbringing for his grandchildren was that they should be 'seen and not heard'. Nevertheless he was a kind man, and he often took my brother and me with him while he drove round his farm in his float.

I remember him as being a tall man, but this is probably because I was a child looking up at him, for he died when I was ten. Certainly he was a very popular man, and as his house was open in welcome to anyone who cared to call there, it was always full of people.

My grandmother, who at that time usually had one or more of her five children living with her, with their husbands or wives, presided over her large and constantly changing household with astonishing calm, and everything ran with the ease of a friendly hotel. A great deal of hard work, however, was needed to give this effect, for there was no electricity, and there were no local shops.

Nearly all our food came from the farm itself. Butter and cheese were made in the dairy, and twice a week the great kitchen would be filled with the unique warm winy smell of bread baking. Here too the hams were smoked, and fruit and vegetables were preserved, and large barrels of good beer were brewed every month for the thirsty farm workers who sat at the long scrubbed tables every day for their dinner.

Although the smells and warmth and friendliness of the kitchen were enticing, I spent very little time there. More exciting things, I felt, were going on outside, in the absorbing world of men.

The stables, of course, drew me most. My grandfather rode to hounds regularly two or three days a week, and he was justly proud of his hunters, which he used to breed with great care and success. I spent hours with the foals, fondling and talking to them, and very gradually being able to distinguish which of them was likely to develop well in conformation.

I did not often see the hunters in action, because although we usually went down to Coedcanlas for Christmas, Father could not stay more than a few days. Douglas, my brother, was for years as a child liable to get tubercular lesions in his lungs if he stayed long near a town, so he lived at the farm, and slept in a summer chalet in the garden. How I envied him his ill health as I was taken home, hearing plans for hunts I would not see, and with the last of the Christmas turkeys not yet picked clean.

In the Easter and summer holidays, my mother and father often sent me alone on the train to Pembrokeshire, under the friendly eye of the guard. I felt immensely important and independent, and I deeply resented the mothering instincts of ladies in railway carriages, though I usually accepted their chocolate. Elderly gentlemen, who either took no notice of me at all, or gravely offered me *The Times* crossword puzzle as a suitable way for a boy of seven to pass a tedious journey, were the companions I approved of.

One winter, however, Father stayed down to enjoy a few weeks' hunting in his native country, and I, theoretically, was to be a companion to my grandmother, who happened at that moment to be living comparatively alone. I neglected her shamefully, for although I was much too small to be mounted, I begged and cajoled every day until someone took me to the meet in a trap or by car.

On rare days the meet was on the other side of the estuary, about six miles from Coedcanlas in a straight line, but almost thirty miles by road and the bridge up the river at Haverfordwest. To avoid the long hack by the land route, it was my grandfather's custom, on reasonably calm days, to take his horses across by boat. He had a large flat-bottomed boat like a ferry, with plenty of room, not only for all his friends and their mounts but for the pack of hounds as well.

The embarkation was a hilarious affair, owing to the steps which had earlier been taken to keep out the cold, but after everyone was safely aboard the boat moved sedately off, and we crossed the mile of water in good style.

In the summer Father sometimes took horses across the estuary to shows, but instead of using the ferry he went over in a rowing boat, and swam the horses across beside him. I went so seldom on these water journeys that they were a great adventure for me, but Father had been doing it all his life, for he, like Mother, was Pembrokeshire born and bred.

They left Wales after the 1914–18 war, when Father returned from France with three pips on his shoulder and no job, and settled down in the Whaddon Chase country, so that Father's abilities in the hunting field and the show ring could be put to good use. He first went to Bishop's, the fashionable hunting stables which was patronized by the Duke of Windsor, then Prince of Wales, and many of his friends, but the yard was burnt down a few years later.

During most of my childhood Father was the manager of W. J. Smith's Hunting Stables at Holyport, near Maidenhead, for after the fire Horace Smith at once asked Father if he would come and work for him.

Horace Smith's Riding School in Cadogan Place, London, was already very well known, and many of the Royal Family were among his pupils and patrons. Smith was also an authority on harness horses, but these having been largely pensioned off by the internal combustion engine, he had decided to open a new stables in the country to deal chiefly in hunters, and he was badly needing someone with expert knowledge to run it for him.

A small yard of about fifteen boxes had been bought, and Father and Horace Smith set off together on a series of journeys all over the country, and to Ireland, to buy suitable horses. Among his other talents Father had a flair for hunters. He knew which to buy, and which to leave alone, and soon Horace Smith relied entirely on Father's judgement, and gave him a free hand with them. Mr Smith was well rewarded. In two years the business had outgrown the small yard to such an extent that the large stables at Holyport was acquired, with its sixty boxes, large paddocks, and its famous indoor riding school.

Here we moved when I was seven, and for the next ten years we lived in the big bungalow beside the yard, where Horace Smith himself lived later. In those days he spent most of his time in London, running his riding school there, and he only came down to Holyport once or twice a week to discuss the business with Father, and to arrange exchanges of horses between the two establishments. Hacks and ponies were at first sent down from London if anyone wanted to hire or buy one in the country, but after the move to Holyport a second riding school was started there, with a good choice of hacks and ponies always on hand. A riding master, Jack Grayston, was appointed, and he was kept very busy.

Although Father dealt with the hacks and ponies as well, his chief interest was always in the hunters, and as he bought young horses, trained, and resold them, he soon built up a reputation for the Stables of having for sale some of the best hunters in England.

I was extremely fortunate in the circumstances of my father's job, and few boys can ever have had more opportunity than I had of learning to ride every possible sort of pony. Father had about eight or nine nagsmen training the hunters under his direction, but they were too big and heavy for young and small ponies, so that Douglas and I had a clear field.

All little boys, I suppose, like to play at doing their father's job, and at first we felt very important when we were allowed to ride the ponies in the yard. As we learned more, though, the make-believe faded away, and riding became for us both a passionate and all-absorbing interest.

Until his health improved when he was about fourteen, Douglas only lived with us at Holyport for short periods, and it was his turn to envy me, as he left me riding the ponies, and went back to his clear sea air.

For me, it was school that was the intolerable interruption

of the serious business of life. I considered the long hours of arithmetic and history a thorough waste of time, and begged every day to be allowed to stay at home. Father did not care whether I went or not, so it was entirely due to Mother's firmness that I attended school at all. Employing some determination and a lot of guile, however, I managed to average only three days a week.

Neither Douglas nor I ever had an official riding lesson. We learned by trial and error, and the errors were liable to be corrected by Father roaring at us from a distance.

'Dick, keep your elbows *in*,' or 'Sit up, boy, sit up.'

Mostly we listened to the riding master when he was teaching other children, and silently followed his advice.

Owing to the number and variety of animals we rode, Douglas and I very soon became fair judges of good and bad ponies. After a while it seemed natural to us to try to correct the faults of the particular pony we were concentrating on, and by the time I was seven or eight I was teaching the bad ponies what the good ponies had already taught me.

Tentatively at first, but with increasing confidence, we would teach a coltish young pony to walk collectedly, or calm a nervous one with quiet talking and fondling, or ride a wicked one hard until it was too tired to play tricks. Gradually, when new ponies came into the yard, Father would say :

'Douglas, hop on this one and see if she is any good.' And sometimes, 'Dick, what sort of a mouth has this old thing got?'

As we progressed also, the riding master used to ask us to give his pupils a lead when they were not doing too well, or to show them how to get their ponies to jump.

I suppose the only thing which saved us from being horribly swollen-headed little boys was the knowledge, drummed into us by Father, the nagsmen, and the ponies themselves, that however much we learned there would always be more to learn. We were never allowed to be satisfied with what we had achieved, never encouraged to think we were any good, always exhorted to greater efforts. I now know that these admonitions, instilled into me at such an early age, were very sensible. Year by year I still find that there is always more to learn, and that it is dangerous to begin to be complacent about one's skill; an unexpected and painful fall is a rough disillusionment.

Douglas and I never owned any of the ponies we rode, so we came to an inevitable parting with all of them. At first I used to be very upset by this continual loss of my dearest friends, but after a while I learned not to lavish on them such a personal and emotional love. I changed, too, from mourning the going of a well-behaved and charming pony, to regretting the departure of a difficult one which still needed a lot of training. I hated to see my job disappearing when it was only half done but, needless to say, when a customer appeared the pony was sold, perfect or not.

From Holyport Mr Smith took some of the best ponies up to his riding school in London, where Her Majesty the Queen and Her Royal Highness Princess Margaret learned to ride. It was a great source of pleasure to me then, and it still is, to reflect that I helped to train several of the ponies which the two Princesses rode when they were children.

The first race I ever won was an apple-bobbing contest at a gymkhana when I was eight, but I regret to say it was not due to the dashing style of my ponymanship in getting to the buckets first. In bed the night before I had been thinking about the best way of getting my teeth into the hard apple floating about on top of the water in the bucket, and had come to a stern conclusion. There was really only one thing to be done.

Next day, therefore, when I threw myself off the pony and on to my knees in front of the pail, I took a deep breath, opened my mouth over the apple, plunged it under my head to the bottom of the bucket, held it there hard, and bit into it. I won the race by minutes, but Mother was not suitably overjoyed at her son's success. She seemed to be more concerned with wringing out the soaking wet collars of my shirt and coat, drying my dripping hair, and prophesying death from pneumonia at an early date.

Her fears were more than ordinary maternal fussing, because I had almost died from pneumonia when I was six months old, and I had caught colds often and easily ever since. With Douglas already a semi-invalid, she was always afraid that her shrimp-sized younger son was hanging on to life by a thread, and the tough constitution which I later developed still surprises her.

From gymkhanas I graduated to the show ring, and in the summer spent every weekday I could wangle from school showing the ponies from W. J. Smith's yard. Round and round and round I went, enjoying myself enormously, while Father did his best at the ringside to sell the pony from under me.

For about ten years horse shows were my summer life, and with all that practice and Father's expert example always before me I had every opportunity to learn how to show a horse or pony to the best advantage. In any case, when I had been at it for a year or two I began to win pony classes and riding classes, and to add my share to the collection of rosettes won by horses and ponies during their brief stay in the yard, and displayed in a glass case in the office. The only rosettes I could keep were those for riding classes; I kept them all in a drawer, for it seemed a little indecent to pin up a lot of round scarlet notices telling me I was 'Best Boy Rider'.

I met Her Majesty the Queen for the first time when I was twelve. It was at Richmond Horse Show, where I had won the riding class and the hunting crop which was its prize. The whip was carefully presented to me by a small girl with an intent expression. I bowed to Princess Elizabeth and thanked her, and she smiled at me; I used the crop for years, and I have it still.

I was very unemotional about the results of pony classes. I won if the pony was good enough and I lost if it was not and, as far as I can remember, without pride in the first case and without jealousy in the second. I suppose this was an echo of Father's professional attitude to showing, for he left me in no doubt that it was always the pony which was being shown, and not me.

Even when I won a riding class he usually greeted me, as I rode out of the ring with the spatter of handclaps warming my heart, with a remark designed to lower any high opinions I might be forming about myself.

'I wouldn't have put you first with your head sticking forward like that,' he would say, or, 'What do you think your heels are for, boy? Use 'em next time.' After a while he would just blow down his nose and say 'Hmph,' a noise indicating in general that I could have done better. Twenty years later, Jack Anthony, winner three times of the Grand National and one of the most famous of all steeplechase jockeys, reminded me of Father in my showing days whenever I had won a race on a horse he had trained. 'You'll learn one day, boy, if you go on trying,' he used to say.

Much though I enjoyed the shows I always looked forward to the end of them, to the crisp winter mornings and the stirring wail of the hunting horn. Hunting was the love of my life.

On school days there were two hazards to be crossed before I could hope to set off behind the hounds. First, I had to persuade Mother that hunting was far more healthy for me than sitting in a stuffy classroom catching other boys' colds, and then to convince her that I was not already running a high temperature. Like many children's, my temperature often rose for no obvious reason, and if Mother saw the slightest flush on my cheeks the thermometer was produced. Such was my success that the school inspector was a regular visitor to the house, and my private consumption of aspirin was phenomenal.

Douglas's ruthless sense of humour sent me out terrified to my very first day's hunting, shortly after my seventh birthday. I had incautiously asked him what 'blooding' meant, as I had heard Father asking the huntsman to blood me on the morrow.

'Oh, it's nothing much,' he said, with awful glee. 'They just cut open the fox's belly and shove your head in.'

The vision of this horror troubled my sleep and ruined the day I had longed for so much, but when the ghastly moment came the huntsman, of course, only smeared his bloody finger gently on my cheek, and gave me the fox's brush.

From then on I thought of little else but the thrills of the chase : my dreams were filled with hedges rushing past me and foxes of super-vulpine speed and cunning streaking ahead of me, and my waking hours were divided between memories of the last hunt and plans for the next one. As I drooped in school over the arithmetic I thought was useless to me, I was thinking, 'I expect they are drawing Ashridge-wood at this very moment' : and as I marched out into the wintry air after lunch to kick a football round a field, I was thinking, 'Perhaps they have just killed at Haines Hill, and they'll be hacking home soon.' As a result, my marks for arithmetic were almost minus, and I cannot to this day kick a ball straight.

Christmas Day suddenly lost its supreme importance in my childish calendar, for after the delights of opening parcels, and the cheerful carol-singing service in church, I was free to attend to the more serious business of Christmas, the business of polishing my saddle and boots until they shone like glass, ready for the year's biggest meet on Boxing Day.

The fascination which hunting held for me had nothing to do with the actual killing of the fox, although that is the only satisfactory ending to a chase : it lay instead in the glorious freedom of making my way across country as fast as I could and as boldly as I dared, in trying on my pony to follow a good horse across the fields and roads I grew to know stick by stone, and in making it a point of honour never to go through a gate if it could be avoided.

Except for the year my grandfather died the alternating pattern of showing and hunting went on unchanged for me until the war interrupted it. My grandmother was left alone in her big house when grandfather died, for all her children were married and had homes and children of their own, and even Douglas had recently outgrown his ill health and had returned to us, so I was sent down to be company for her. I lived with her for nearly a year, and my uncles and aunts and cousins came in turn to visit her, but they were quiet and sad days for us all. The house seemed like a shell of walls listening to the bustle and noise of the past, and it was not only the withdrawal of Grandfather's dominant personality that was grieving us, but also the awareness that for our family an era had come to an end.

The farm was to be sold. Grandfather had left it to his children, but none of his three sons could buy out his brothers and sisters, and none of them really wanted to take on Coedcanlas, for farming was not a booming industry in the early 1930s.

To my disgust my education went on, and I walked the two miles each day to the little two-roomed schoolhouse in Lawrenny village,

> 'with . . . satchel and shining morning face
> creeping like snail unwillingly to school.'

I would never have believed that I would be so eager to go to school that I would slip off early without anyone noticing me, and run for half a mile with many glances over my shoulder to make sure no one was following me : and if you suppose that the alternative if I stayed at home was extremely unpleasant, you are quite right. There was one job on the farm which was usually done by a boy, and I happened to be the only one there. It was to clear the corn dust away from under the threshing machine, a job I hated. Even school was a kinder fate, but alas, on the days I reached that haven unobserved someone was sent to haul me out of the classroom and back to my post. The threshing went on for about a week, and after that my views of school returned to normal.

On the faithful old donkey I made my last melancholy journeys round the well-loved fields, along the estuary, and through the woods, with the desperate feeling of a child that the foundations of my life were slipping away, and that nothing would ever be the same again.

Once I was home, however, and back to my ponies, I rapidly shed my sadness and eagerly took up the old routine of hunting, showing, and avoiding going to school.

When I was twelve I missed a whole summer term. After Easter Mother sent me to the dentist for my holiday check-up, and he said I needed a brace for my teeth. The two incisors which had helped me so admirably in the apple-bobbing race were now dominating my face : they were splendid, large, and white, but I could hardly shut my mouth over them. I went one Saturday morning and was measured for the brace which would draw them in a little.

In the afternoon, in the covered riding school, I rode a nervous highly bred show pony called Tulip round and round, in an attempt to quieten and calm her. There came a moment when I wanted her to go one way and she wanted to go another and, as temperamental animals sometimes do when they are crossed, she stood straight up on her hind legs in fury. Unfortunately she overbalanced and fell over backwards on top of me. The pommel of the saddle landed on my face.

I cannot remember much of what happened next; I awoke some time later in hospital, very sore and quite unable to speak. My two big teeth would need a brace no longer, for they had been retrieved by the surgeon from somewhere behind my nose. My upper jaw, palate, and nose were broken in several places, and I was altogether a depressing sight. Everything mended quickly, however, and I was still young enough for the large gap in front of my mouth to close slowly up as my other teeth moved round into the space.

My smashed face was an excellent reason for a prolonged absence from school, although I was back in the show ring as soon as my skin had healed, and before I could talk properly again. The doctors earned my heartfelt thanks by telling Mother that I was not fit enough to return to Maiden-

head Grammar School, and that I should be sent in the
autumn to a smaller, quieter place. There was no inspector
to check on my attendance at the private school Mother
chose, so I went less than ever.

My accident on Tulip led to great adventures, for when
he saw that I was going to be able to go to all the summer
shows without classroom interruption, the great Bertram
Mills asked Father to let me ride his show ponies for him.
Father agreed, and I was ecstatic.

Bertram Mills took a great delight in showing his many
horses and ponies and in seeing them win prizes for jumping,
and all the summer, while his circus with its highly trained
liberty horses and its lolloping rosinbacks was on its pro-
vincial tour, he devoted himself to his hobby horses at the
shows. As far as I knew, he never showed a circus pony, or
trained a show pony for the circus, but always kept his two
interests apart.

He was as familiar a figure at shows as at the circus, a
cheerful man with a shining bald head, the former under-
taker who conjured up romance and glitter for millions of
children. He sent me all over England to shows with his
ponies, and I usually travelled in the railway horse-box with
them, sleeping on a bunk beside them on long journeys, and
looking after them on the way.

One time, the first summer, Bertram Mills sent me to
jump a pony at Southport Show in Lancashire. We were
there for two or three days, just too long for my meagre
pocket money to withstand the tug of the nearby fun-fair,
and then we went back overnight to Bertram Mills' home
at Chalfont St Giles. I spent the morning there jumping the
other ponies, then Mr Mills said, 'Thank you, Dick. You'd
better be off home now.'

Home. Father had driven me over, but was not coming
to take me back, and my bus fare had vanished on the
swings and roundabouts at Southport. Blushing, I explained
my financial crisis to Mr Mills, and asked him to lend me
half a crown.

'I never carry any change,' he said, 'so I haven't half a

crown.' He brought a piece of white paper out of his trouser pocket. 'You'd better take this. I don't want it back.' It was a crisp new five-pound note, the first I had ever owned.

I climbed on to the bus clutching my treasure tightly, very sorry I should so soon have to part with it; but when I offered it to the conductor for my half fare to Slough, he could not change it. I travelled to Slough free. On the next bus, and the next, the same thing happened, and I went all the way home without paying, just because I had too much money.

Every Christmas Mr Mills gave me and my family tickets for his circus, and every January I spent fruitless hours trying to stand up on a pony's narrow rump while it cantered round in a circle. The pony unfortunately had not been to the circus and took most unkindly to its new role. By February each year I had decided after all not to be a mounted acrobat in spangled tights bursting through a paper hoop, and had renounced my ambitions to drive two horses with one foot on the back of each.

My first appearance in hunter classes at horse shows was a case of life following closely in the well-worn traditions of Boy's Paper fiction.

Father was planning to show a horse at the Islington Royal Agricultural Show in the lightweight hunter class. On the eve of the show Father was suddenly stricken with sciatica and could hardly walk. This was a serious blow to the owner of Ballymonis, the horse which Father was due to ride, for conformation alone will not win a hunter class. The horse has to be presented in the best way to the judges so that they notice him and see how he moves, and it takes practice to do this. Father's skill in the show ring was outstanding, so that finding a substitute for him at such short notice was no simple matter.

'Dick can ride him,' said Father, when all other suggestions had been turned down.

At the show, the news that I was to ride Ballymonis was received with some consternation in hunter-class circles. Mr

Bernard Selby, the horse's owner, looked at me sideways.

'He's very small,' he said to Father in a doubtful voice. It was indeed true, for although I was then fourteen I still weighed only five stone.

'It's dangerous,' said a friend of Father's. 'The horse is wild. It'll run away with him.'

Ballymonis had a habit of taking charge and ignoring his rider's wishes, and had once at Richmond jumped straight out of the ring, but I had ridden him at home and with youthful confidence had no doubt that all would be well.

So round I went on my full-sized and high-spirited hunter, and Ballymonis, a sweet and beautiful horse, won his class. Mr Selby was so pleased that he gave me a new suit and an overcoat. Father's sciatica got better, but he let me help him often in hunter classes after that; and I grew in experience.

I had hoped to leave school on the day the law allowed, the day after my fourteenth birthday, but Mother insisted that I was still too young and would not let me leave for more than another year. Of course she was right, but at the time I did not think so.

TWO

Rings and Wings

While many little boys were driving the Scottish Express round their nurseries, my rocking horse and I were going over Becher's and Valentine's, the Chair and the Canal Turn. The names of the fences at Liverpool were a chant, an invocation, a beckoning magic, and the spell they laid on me in my infancy has never been broken. Now that I know them so very well, and have a hundred memories of their hazards and glories in every sort of weather, their names have an even stronger evocative power, for I remember them with a more intense pleasure than ever I imagined them.

If it is possible to inherit so vague a quality as a wish to be a jockey, I did so. My father was a jockey, and his father also.

My grandfather, Willie Francis, and his half-brother Robert Harries, were two of the best amateur riders of their generation, and from 1885 to about 1905 they won every possible point-to-point and amateur 'chase in the then flourishing centre of south-west Wales. Robert Harries was the Master of the Carmarthenshire Hounds, and he and Willie Francis filled in the gaps between races by hunting. Any pursuit which did not involve riding was, in their opinion, a waste of time.

Willie Francis was crippled in early middle age by arthritis, and had to give up riding and farming. From then on he left to his wife most of the burden of directing their three grown sons and young daughter into good careers. Of all their children, Father was the only one who insisted that horses were to be his life, and his mother, because he pestered her to let him and because she did not realize that such a job would prevent him ever riding as an amateur, agreed that he should join the racing stable of Col Lort Phillips at Lawrenny. There, to the stable that had recently sent Kirkland to win the Grand National, he went when he was sixteen, and Col Lort Phillips soon took out a licence for him to ride in races.

Father enjoyed his first years there immensely and rode in and won many races, but as time went by it became clear that as long as he stayed there he had no hope of ever being more than the stable jockey second string to the brilliant Tich Mason, who rode regularly for Lort Phillips and was the leading jockey of his day.

The events of 1914 ended the stalemate and sent Father to France. He was by then secretly engaged to Mother, but her father disapproved of the match, and finally gave his consent to it only when Father agreed not to return to racing. They were married in 1915, on one of Father's rare leaves at home.

Brought up on tales of my father's and grandfather's prowess, and with their blood in my small veins, it was no wonder that I got it firmly into my head in early childhood that I was going to be a jockey too. The sense that my future was already determined underlay everything I did from the day I rode the donkey backwards. I did not yearn to start racing, or even think about it a great deal, but to everyone who asked me what I was going to be when I grew up I answered, 'A jockey.'

For a long while it seemed possible that I was going to be small enough for flat racing. Mother and Father's feelings were mixed : they realized that successful flat-race jockeys make a good income, but they disliked the idea of my being an apprentice, and they wanted a normal-sized son.

A friend of Father's, Herbert Rich, who was interested in breeding and hunting and had horses in training, kept urging Father to send me to Stanley Wootton's stable at Epsom. Stanley Wootton, a great friend of his, was then supreme in turning apprentices into first-class jockeys.

Bert Rich often surveyed my small person, and one day

turned to Father and said, 'Give him gin, lad, give him gin. That'll keep him from growing.'

Mother gave me milk, however, and like Alice in Wonderland I suddenly started to grow at an enormous rate, shooting up into a long and stringy shape quite unsuited and much too heavy for flat racing. No one was unduly disturbed by my mushroom performance, for steeplechasing had really been my aim all along : just as well, for I grew eighteen inches in less than four years before I slowed down to a more reasonable rate.

After a left school I became a sort of extension of Father. When he wanted to be in two places at once, or riding two horses at once, I was his other self. I went on riding and training the horses in W. J. Smith's yard with the nagsmen as I had done since I was seven, and hunted and showed dozens and dozens of them. In the winter we hunted with the Garth always two and sometimes four days a week, and on Fridays we went out with the Berks and Bucks Farmers' Staghounds.

Many of the people who bought hunters from the stables lived too far away for a horse to be boxed to them in the morning in time for the meet, so when they were wanting to buy another horse and wished to see how it would perform in the field it had to be taken over the day before.

'I'll send my boy over with the horse,' Father used to tell them.

I always enjoyed those journeys. Father sent me off in a horse-box, sitting beside the driver, with a groom, and perhaps two horses for the buyer to choose from, and it never occurred to me at all that anyone would think that at fifteen I was rather young for the job.

When we arrived at our host's house I used to show the horse to its prospective owner, and the next morning rode it with the hounds. If there were two horses, I rode one and the buyer the other, and we exchanged horses during the day so that he could see both of the horses in action and find out which of them gave him the best ride. If one of the horses was suitable I left it with him, and went home again with the other.

In that way I hunted many days with the Bicester, Whaddon Chase, Pytcheley, Cottesmore, Duke of Beaufort's, Belvoir, Atherstone, and Meynell packs, and many others as well. Of them all the Meynell was my favourite, not because the country was the best for hunting, but because the fields were small and the fences round them large; and while we enjoyed ourselves jumping them the foxes were welcome to live a little longer.

About a year after I had left school I asked Father to help me get a job as a junior assistant and general factotum in a steeplechasing stable, so that I could start to ride as an amateur jockey. Mother disapproved of my ambitions, and Father was not enthusiastic, but he agreed to do his best. He took me with him to see Gwynne Evans, who was then training at Druid's Lodge for Mr J. V. Rank, and whom Father knew well from the days when they were boys together in South Wales.

The day we spent there made me keener than ever to race and quite sure that nothing would ever change my mind about it. Gwynne Evans said he would take me, but not for a year.

'You are still a bit too young,' he said. 'Come when you are seventeen.'

Disappointed though I was at the delay, his promise that I could go with him in a year was like a light at the end of a tunnel. A year seemed a very long time to me when I was sixteen, and I thought as I drove home beside Father in a silent mixture of gloom and delight that it would never pass.

In a way, it never did.

For more than six months everything I planned seemed to have a temporary quality, for all the time I was thinking to myself, 'This time next year . . .' I lived in and for that distant time, and Father and Mother were getting used to the idea of my going. Then one day they broke to me the news that Gwynne Evans was dead. He had been killed in a car crash.

After a month or two Father wrote to Ivor Anthony, whom he had also known as a boy and fellow jockey, asking him if he needed a very junior assistant. Ivor Anthony, trainer of two Grand National winners, wrote back encouragingly, but said he had no vacancy at that moment as he already had two assistants. He hinted, however, that Evan Williams, who was then riding for him as an amateur, would soon be turning professional, and when that happened he would consider adding me to his stable.

With this much vaguer prospect and more timeless wait I had to be as content as I could, for although Father wrote to one or two more friends the answer was always the same. 'He is still too young.' 'He is only sixteen, there's plenty of time.'

It seemed unreasonable to me then that my age in years should matter so much. I felt mentally grown up, and I was physically growing too. I did not think that at seventeen, eighteen or nineteen I would have changed a great deal, and I urgently felt that plenty of time was just what I had not got.

It was at about this time that Father and Mother decided to leave Smith's and start a similar business of their own. For years they had been talking of having their own stables, but had never taken the plunge into uncertainty. It is no small thing for a man to take and risk all the family's capital for the sake of personal independence when he is in an interesting and safe job. The snag about this particular job was, however, that it was not well paid, and Mother eventually began to search seriously for a suitable house for us to move to. She found the ideal place in Embrook House, near Wokingham, a large, pleasant, Victorian house with a good stable yard of about twenty-five boxes.

We made the move early in 1938, and from then on it was impossible for me to leave and go racing, even if anyone would have had me. I worked harder than I had ever done before, doing in earnest what for ten years had been a pleasant pastime and helping Father in whatever way I could to make a success of his new business.

The stables at Embrook were small compared with Smith's at Holyport, but they prospered steadily just the same. Mother was the backbone and mainstay of the whole undertaking. She ran the large house and gave us all encouragement, and took in and saw to the welfare of a succession of pupils learning stable management.

Ever since I could remember Mother had a deep interest in antique furniture and all the male members of her family suffered from it now and then.

'Dick,' she called out of the window one day. 'Come in and help your father with this chest.'

I went in and found Father struggling to lift one end of an enormous chest of drawers which had for months been an undisturbed part of the hall furniture. After half an hour's strenuous effort we managed between us to get the chest upstairs into the new space Mother had planned for it. While we mopped our brows and flexed our cracking muscles Mother looked at the chest from all angles.

'No,' she said, 'it doesn't look right there at all. It'll have to go down into the hall again.'

This sort of thing happened often. My father, brother, uncles and I all became expert furniture removers.

Mother's hobby was attending auction sales in remote farmhouses. She had a theory that treasures were likely to be found where they had grown old with a house, and that the farmers who owned them might not realize their quality. She had an eye as sharp as any antique dealer's, and from time to time I came into the house to find her fondly regarding some painted monstrosity which I might well have chopped up for firewood.

'Eighteenth century,' she would say with approval, or 'Satinwood under all that paint.' Away would go the object to be stripped, and back would come a beautiful and delicate table or chair or writing desk. She could probably tell from running her hand down the legs of a piece of furniture as much about its worth as Father could from doing the same to a horse, for she often showed me how new legs and backs had been joined to antique fronts and tops, and remarked that the underpinnings must be in good shape whether it is a chair or a horse one wishes to sit on.

The size and number of the rooms at Embrook House were a delight and challenge to her, and she gradually filled them with her discovered treasures. Her discernment was well known in 'the trade', and one London store asked her to go every week and arrange their window display of antiques. She would have loved to have accepted, but her variable health could not be guaranteed to be always good on Mondays.

We settled down so comfortably and quickly at Embrook that after a year or so my mind was straying again towards racing. I could not now leave Father for National Hunt steeplechasing, but there was still the possibility of point-to-points. The trouble was that Father's horses stayed such a short time in the yard that I could not qualify them for point-to-points by hunting them eight times, even if Father had agreed to my risking their valuable necks in races, so I had to trust to an invitation from friends. Quite understandably, they did not ask me when they could get someone who had done it before.

To my joy, however, in the autumn of 1938 Oliver Dixon, a horse dealer of renown and a family friend, asked me to ride all his horses in point-to-points in the following spring. I hunted his horses during the winter, but as the time drew near for the first point-to-point Oliver Dixon died.

Deeply disappointed, I was again an onlooker at the races, with such envy and longing to be taking part myself that they held no pleasure for me.

Then came the war.

Slowly as it started, hunting as slowly declined, and the next year's point-to-point races were cancelled. Father's business began to dwindle, for with the future uncertain fewer people wanted to buy horses, and there was gradually less and less for me to do at home.

Early in 1940 I told my father and mother that I was just off to join the cavalry. But the cavalry, I was downhearted to discover, did not want me. It seemed that to get into the cavalry I should have to wait until my age group was called up, and then trust to luck.

I went home and wrote to two friends in the Scots Greys at Edinburgh begging their help, and a few days later returned to the recruiting office armed with letters of introduction and a request that I should be dispatched to Edinburgh by the next train, breeched and spurred for action.

The recruiting officer was aggressively unimpressed. No strings, his cold glance said, were going to be pulled while he was there to prevent it. Declining his invitation to sign on as an assistant cook in the infantry, I went out into the street, defeated and depressed.

I stood outside the door of the recruiting centre, aimlessly looking up at the pale sunshine in the early spring sky, and on an impulse turned round and went in again for a third attempt. I tried a different man at a different table, but he had the same bored, unfriendly eyes.

'I want to fly,' I said.

'Air-gunner,' he said. It was a statement, not a question.

'No,' I said, 'a pilot.'

'Air-gunner or ground staff,' he replied, 'we're not taking anything else.'

'Pilot.' I was firm.

He looked at me more coldly than ever. Then he said, 'You can sign on for a trade, and then re-muster for flying when you are in.'

It was my first experience of the easy callous lying of the forces, and I did not recognize it. I believed him, and I signed on as an airframe fitter.

When I tried to re-muster I was laughed at for being so simple.

'An airframe fitter you signed on as,' they said, 'and an airframe fitter you'll stay.' And with rage in his heart, an airframe fitter was what 922385 AC2 Francis R. became.

Regularly every month I sent in an application to be transferred to flying school : and regularly every month I got no reply. I learned how to clean, grease, take apart, put together, and mend every inch of an aeroplane except the engine itself, and I loathed it.

After a year I was called in for an interview. It was strongly pointed out to me that as I had already received one sort of training it was a waste of the country's time and money to give me another. I protested bitterly that I had never wanted and had tried to avoid the first training, but to no avail. I was sent back to airframes.

After a while I went on a ten-week voyage via the mid-Atlantic to Egypt, and spent two years or so chasing backwards and forwards in the desert. When the army was advancing we moved up behind it on to airfields which had been bombed by our air force and blown up by the retreating Italians, and we got used to living in ruins and making workshops in the rubble. When the army was retreating we fell back to the now repaired and efficient airfields behind us, but as we were bombed by night and day we spent a good deal of our time in slit trenches, still unable to enjoy the comfort of the newly built huts. After the enemy had bombed the airfield for a few days and we had blown up what we could not take, we hurried eastwards again, leaving everything very much as we had found it on our advance.

In both directions we patched and mended the torn bodies of the planes as they landed, getting them back into the air again as soon as we could. I acquired the sleeve propeller of an LAC and a lifelong distaste for sand. And every month I sent in my application to fly.

Every six months I was given an interview, but it was only a formality : airframe fitters, it seemed, were scarcer than pilots.

At every interview I was asked what my hobbies were, as there was a space on the interviewer's papers for this vital information. I tried each time to think of some really impressive hobby which would convince the board of my air-mindedness, but bird-watching, kite-flying, and star-gazing had not moved them. Eventually, and with nothing to lose, I fell back on the truth.

A rather peppery Squadron Leader consulted his notes.

'Well – er – er – Francis. What are your hobbies?'

'Huntin', shootin', and fishin', sir,' I said.

The Squadron Leader exploded. 'Get out of here at once,' he said. 'I'll have none of your bloody cheek.'

And that was that.

Whenever we got a few days leave from our desert life the lights of Cairo attracted us like moths, and although on longer leaves I hitchhiked to Jerusalem and Tel Aviv, to Beirut and Damascus, most of my holidays were spent beside the Nile.

Here one day, when several of us went to inspect the Pyramids, we saw a line of mangy-looking camels holding their supercilious noses in the air. It appeared that they were for hire, rather like donkeys on the sands at Bognor, complete with a dirty burnous'd Arab to help intrepid customers to mount and to run along beside the camel for the first few yards, shouting advice to both animal and rider in a totally unintelligible local tongue.

We paid our piastres and took our choice, and started off over the burning sands of Egypt. As a form of transport a camel is very uncomfortable indeed. It rocks and sways, pitches and dips, and its trotting action on the way back was nearly my undoing, for the Ship of the Desert was rapidly making me seasick, and it would be better to draw a yashmak over the whole proceeding.

The battle of El Alamein was won, and we made our way for the third time across the Libyan desert. The Germans had blown up everything even more thoroughly than the Italians and the RAF had, and the airfields could barely be distinguished from the rest of the desolate country except for the enormous bomb craters and the concentrations of ruined buildings, trucks and aircraft to be found there. As before we made our home in the rubble, but in good spirits because we were going in the right direction again.

When the end of the North African campaign was in sight, and my thirty-seventh application form was on its way to the wastepaper basket, the CO sent for me.

'Francis,' he said, 'Group HQ say they are tired of seeing

your name every month. They give in. You're to report to
Suez for transport to Rhodesia.'

At last, when I had almost given up hope, I was going to
learn the one and only thing I still did not know about an
aeroplane : how to fly it. I left the drab and dirty desert with
barely a backward glance.

Flying was everything I had imagined it to be, and from
the moment I climbed into the open cockpit of a Tiger
Moth behind the instructor I began to enjoy life again. The
lightness of our little craft as it lifted off the ground and the
rushing air round my head seemed to slough off the years
of grime and drudgery, and ten flying hours later, when I
went up on my first solo, I felt exhilarated and whole. In
solo flying, once I had passed the stage of worrying all the
time I was in the air whether I would get safely down, I
found again what Service life denies, the blessed peace of
being alone.

On the ground, life was more crowded than ever. The
arithmetic I had not learned at school reproached me when
I attacked the problems of navigation, and I found it was
not very easy to work out a route to a distant spot on an
imaginary longitude when I ran out of fingers to add up
with. Every hour was filled by lectures on meteorology,
signals, theory of flying, navigation, standard procedure
and other mysteries, but at the end of it all a year later I
was sent back to England with a certificate saying I was
fit to fly fighter aircraft.

The invasion of Europe had begun, and the big bombing
raids were being launched from this country, so that at first
I flew on fighter escort duty. Soon it was clear that there
was very little for us to fight, and the Empire Training
Scheme having trained thousands more fighter pilots than
were by then needed, I was transferred from Spitfires to
Bomber Command, given some minimum instructions, and
sent up in a Wellington bomber. I and three others were in
fact used as guinea pigs to discover how quickly a fighter
pilot could be trained for bombers, but I did not like the
change at all.

Aerobatics in a single-engined aircraft had been an essential part of our fighter training, and I had always enjoyed the easy lift and the quick manœuvrability of the little machines in rolls and spins and side-slips. There could be no such fun with a Wellington. They seemed heavy and sluggish to me, and the simplest turn took three times as much time and effort. Even in very cold weather I was always sweating from exertion by the time I had got my Wellington home.

In later years some weary old three-mile steeplechasers hung on my arms in much the same way; and the likeness of different types of horses to aircraft is not as unnoticed by the RAF as one might think. When I had finished my first hour's flying lesson, the instructor asked me what my civilian job had been. I explained that I had done little but ride horses.

'Good,' he said. 'We always find that people who can ride learn to fly easily. Something to do with having good hands, and you need light hands on a fighter aircraft. Treat the Tiger Moth like a horse with a tender mouth, and you won't go far wrong.'

The Wellingtons from the station I was on were making diversionary air attacks on Europe to cover the real aim of the main bombing forces, and although we did not know it until the next day, we were doing that for the Dam-Busters too, on the night they breached the Mohne and Eder dams.

During the coldest part of the winter I was sent on a short course to learn how to fly the heavy troop-carrying gliders that were to take our army across the Rhine. In between wrestling with landing these cumbersome engineless craft we were given an intensive infantry assault training on the freezing wastes of Salisbury Plain, for after we had landed our load of soldiers the glider pilots were to get out and fight with the army. We were chivvied and chased through the course by a tough and disillusioned sergeant-major, who could often be heard yelling with sadistic pleasure :

'Lie down on your stomachs in the snow. Now wriggle forward a hundred yards. The enemy is looking at you.

Keep your flaming head down ... sir.' And he gloomily foretold that not only would we all kill ourselves by our own stupidity but that we would be a nuisance and a risk to all 'proper' soldiers.

I was not at all looking forward to marching across Germany on my stomach, but the Rhine was crossed with less trouble than had been expected. Only twenty courses of glider-trained pilots were needed, and I was on course twenty-two.

It was a great relief to me to be back in my heavy Wellington; at least I had the comfort of knowing that it would go up as well as down.

As the war drew to its close in Europe we had less and less to do, until my crew and I were transferred to Coastal Command to help in the escorting into British ports of surrendering German warships and merchantmen. We acted almost as air policemen on traffic duty, partly making sure the vessels were not heading for trouble in mine-fields, and partly seeing that they continued on the course which had been given them and did not change their minds about turning themselves in. It meant long hours of flying over the sea and very little for the crew to do. The bomb-aimer and the air-gunner read *Men Only*, the navigator and the radio-operator checked the ships and our position and reported back to base, and they all called me 'the chauffeur' and made disparaging remarks about the hours of sun-bathing I was putting in in the cockpit. I used to lie back in my seat, flying on course by the instruments, with nothing to do but look at the sky above and the occasional ship below. But one day as I sat there relaxing comfortably another aircraft flew over the top of us so close that if it had lowered its undercarriage it would have landed on us, and after that I always sat up and looked where I was going.

When all the escort duty was done we were still flying daily over the North Sea, but now with navigators who had just finished their lessons on the ground and were in need of practice in the air. My job was to fly them out over the sea and let them direct me home. If they made a mistake I had to remember what it was and also know how to get back to our own airfield should we arrive in error at John o' Groats; and as a good deal of this navigator training was at night, and I had learned my navigation by the Southern Cross, I was sometimes a bit lost myself. Luckily, however, I had been stationed at almost every airfield in Great Britain and knew the ground plan of most of them from the air, so I never actually made the awful blunder of landing at the wrong one.

If it had not been for radio communication from aircraft to base, and the 'beam' system which guided us in to the runways, the enormous amount of night flying done by the RAF would have been quite impossible, for without such help it is a hopeless task to find one particular square mile in a moonless blacked-out country.

With the ending of the Far Eastern war the slow business of demobilization began, but Father wanted me home to help him as soon as it could be managed, so I applied for a compassionate release.

Meanwhile, to keep us occupied, the RAF went on sending pilots and crews to learn to fly the heavy four-engined Lancaster bombers. I sat in the co-pilot's seat beside the instructor, helplessly looking at the banks and banks of round instrument faces, control buttons, and fuel gauges, wishing I could spend my last weeks in the air flying my first loves, the superb Spitfires. But Lancasters it was, and I flew them until I left.

From Tiger Moths to Lancasters, I never lost a deep feeling of pleasure when the nose of an aircraft came up as we were airborne, the satisfaction of nursing an engine to its highest efficiency, or the buoyancy and freedom of the long hours in the sky.

In the late autumn of 1945 I went to the wedding of my cousin Nesta.

I had promised to be best man if I could get leave and, everything being well, I set off with Mother on the train to Weston-super-Mare, I with my mind back in my Wellington cockpit at Silverstone and Mother chatting about which of our relations were going to the wedding too. Nothing warned me, as we trundled through Somerset in the peaceful October sunshine, of the emotional whirlwind that was waiting for me.

Mother and I were greeted and fussed over by my aunt and cousins and a large contingent of relatives, so that it was some time before I noticed a stranger standing back a little shyly from our family reunion. A girl in a brown dress, with pale gold hair.

My aunt said, 'Dick, I don't think you have ever met Mary. She is a friend of Nesta's who has come for the wedding.'

Mary and I smiled at each other and to my astonishment, before we had even spoken, I found myself thinking, 'This is my wife.'

I had never believed in love at first sight and it still seems to me an unreasonable way of choosing a companion for life, but there it was in a flash between us, and our future was pledged in a glance.

THREE

Under Starter's Orders

The war had changed me.

I made this not very original but personally disturbing discovery during the first few months after my return home.

Through all the difficult years, with only one groom to help him, and struggling to feed the horses properly on poor and hardly obtained fodder, Father had kept his business going with the sole idea that I should have something to come home to. He and Mother certainly had every reason to believe that I would take over from them and, with the return of more normal conditions, rebuild their once flourishing concern. For years I had not referred to my old desire to be a jockey, and I had even half convinced myself that hunting and showing were satisfying occupations after all.

I worked very hard for Father, glad that he could at last have some rest. Our Irish groom, the only one left, had too much work to manage by himself, so I often found myself cleaning out the stables, sweeping the yard, and cleaning the tack, as well as my intended job of riding and training the horses which Father bought and sold for the hunting field and the show ring. Father had also acquired two or three horses at livery which had to be groomed and saddled for their owners' visits, and several child pupils who came regularly for riding lessons.

Mary came down to stay with us for the weekend every two or three weeks. Later she said to some friends, 'My courtship was spent leaning over the bottom halves of stable doors while Dick mucked out an endless row of horses.

'And,' she added with a grin, 'on Sunday afternoons we sat in the tack-room while he washed a mountain of dirty leather.'

Whenever I had a weekend free I went up to Denbigh-shire to see Douglas, who was then estate manager to Mr Victor Dyke Dennis, and to my great delight Douglas's father-in-law, Bob Thelwell, let me ride his horse in two local point-to-points.

Although these efforts were not spectacularly successful, Douglas persuaded Mr Dennis to let me ride one of his horses also, in a point-to-point, and I later rode the same horse in a hunter 'chase at Bangor-on-Dee. My first appearance on a real racecourse passed unnoticed by the general public, I am glad to say. It was not a very distinguished performance, but we finished the course and I went back to the daily routine at home with something to think about while I carried the hay and cut the chaff.

I did not in the least mind being kept continually busy, because I have always found idleness very hard to bear, but my troubles started with the showing season. Before the war I had always enjoyed the enormous amount of showing which came my way on account of Father's occupation, but now I found I disliked it.

The change was in me. After six years of an existence when on occasions even life itself was from minute to minute uncertain, the opinion of two men on which of six horses was the best shape seemed to me to be so unimportant as to be ridiculous.

Where once I had felt friendly rivalry and good-humoured competition, I now saw vanity, malice, and jealousy; and as the long summer programme wore on, from hunter trials to the big county shows, I became more and more convinced that I could not spend the rest of my life in the showing and horse-dealing world.

Now that I am securely outside that world, and un-touched by its politics and prejudices, I enjoy meeting old friends on the few occasions that I go back. At Finmere, for the last few years, there has been a Jockeys' Speed Jumping Competition, which we all enjoy and look forward to. It is a light-hearted affair which causes great amusement to the crowd, who sense that it is a holiday performance and expect all the jockeys to make fools of themselves in their strange environment.

Usually, we oblige.

One year I was mounted on a horse that suffered from a chronic inability to lift its hind legs, so that we left a trail of fallen gates, bars and bricks behind us, and scored a record number of faults for the course. Another year, I fell off and dislocated my shoulder : an embarrassment to me, and the cause of much ribald comment from everybody. Any poor jockey mounted on a green horse or a bad jumper is greeted with yells of laughter and derision as he makes his disastrous way round from jump to jump, losing his hat, whip, balance, reputation and composure as he goes.

Several times, in the last few years, I have been asked to judge some hunter classes, and I always enjoy this, feeling safe from accusations of favouritism as nearly always the horses and riders are unknown to me. My ability as a judge may reasonably be doubted, but at least no one can say :

'Oh, of course he has put Mr So-and-so's horse first. After all, he sold it to him.' Or :

'He has only given Such-and-such first prize because it was put first at Blank Show, and he wants to flatter the judge there.'

Remarks like these, unjust and prompted by jealousy and disappointment though they were, were so common in my ears during that first summer after the war that I was sickened and stifled by the whole atmosphere.

I began to feel that the only satisfactory judge of a horse was the winning post. First there, I thought, and no arguments.

The old impulse to be a jockey grew stronger. As the months went by, it became irresistible. Space, I said to myself as I cantered round in small circles; speed, I whispered, as I slowly popped over the jumps; stamina, I thought, as I eyed the fat nags lined up beside me.

Although I had, I suppose, a somewhat romantic idea of racing, leaving the rails of the show ring for those of the paddock was for me a liberation and a fulfilment. As I have grown older I have discovered, of course, that in every profession one has to bear public humiliations and private heartaches, and that no competitive job is free of some wry and wistful regret for lost opportunities. Nevertheless, I have always been glad that I did at last become a jockey, and I can truthfully say that there was nothing else on earth I would rather have done.

In the summer of 1946, however, I still had to find some way of putting into practice my strengthening resolve to ride in races, and I could remember only too well the lack of success I had had before the war when I had tried to get myself adopted by a trainer.

Again I wrote to every trainer I had ever met, or who had ever met my parents, and on more distant acquaintance-ship even than that, but all I had back were polite letters saying that no one had a post suitable for a totally in-experienced amateur jockey. One could hardly blame them.

Mother and Father were equally discouraging, but from different motives. Mother frankly said that she would always be worrying about my safety, that I had no idea how ruthless the racing world is, and that she wished I would be content to carry on with Father's business.

Father said that being a jockey was a very uncertain occupation, that the chances of making a good living at it were small, and that I would do much better altogether to stick to what I was doing. All their advice was good, but I could not take it, even though I was aware of several more difficulties besides inexperience which would have to be overcome.

I was already twenty-five, almost too old to start a job which inevitably retires one at forty, when the body can no longer easily stand the constant strain and injury; and I needed a salary, however small, so that I could use my small capital for my racing expenses and remain an amateur jockey for some time.

There were so many advantages in starting as an amateur that I did not even consider taking out a licence, getting a stable job, and hoping for a few chance rides to come my way. It is easy to get a job like that, but the chance rides are few and far apart, and the proportion of successful jockeys who have started in that way is very small. Many jockeys were apprenticed as boys in flat-racing stables and turned to hurdling and steeplechasing when they grew too heavy for the flat, and many others started as amateurs, as I was hoping to do.

After months of alternate hope and depression, I heard one day from Douglas, who had been doing his best for me in the North, that George Owen would take me on as his secretary. George, who had been a first-rank jockey and had won the Cheltenham Gold Cup in 1939, was farming and training a few horses, and the two jobs between them left him very little time for all the office work which had to be done.

'Dick,' he said to Douglas, 'can come and sort this lot out if he likes.' And he pointed to a heap of bills, forms, racing calendars and unopened letters.

Dick was absolutely delighted to be given the chance.

I had only met George once, when he stayed with us before the war for a night between race meetings, but I had often seen him racing and had always admired his horsemanship. I was sure, though, that he could not remember me, and was only taking me on Douglas's account, so I was doubly keen not to disgrace myself either as a secretary, or as a jockey, when I rode one of his horses in a race.

He had agreed to pay me a few pounds a week for my services, and I was to live in his house as one of the family. With everything settled at last, I parted from my still faintly disapproving parents, and in October set off on the train for Cheshire and the unknown future, feeling like a small boy going to a new school.

The warmth of the welcome that George and his wife Margot gave me at once dispelled my feelings of strangeness, and their family of small girls soon made me feel at home. At that time George had a dairy farm a few miles from Chester, and his hospitality and the bustle of the farm kitchen reminded me vividly of my childhood at Coedcanlas.

George's parents and brothers and sisters all lived fairly near and Margot's large family were not much farther away, and they and their friends were constantly visiting each other's houses for company or to play cards. All these people seemed to accept as a matter of course that I, as a part of George's household, should be invited too, so in a very few weeks I had become part of the social landscape and had made several lasting friendships. Cheshire must surely be among the friendliest of counties, for although I only lived there for three years in all, I know more people there than in any other place, and when I go there now to race meetings it is like going home.

George had not exaggerated when he told me that his racing accounts were not in order. As I settled down to his desk, I discovered that he had not sent out a single bill for training fees for almost six months. He had paid all the bills which corn merchants, horse-box hire firms, blacksmiths and saddlers had sent him, but had not kept any record of them, and when I sorted out the large pile of receipts it became clear that many of them were missing.

I set to work to restore some order to the huge muddle, and by studying 'chasing records to find out which horses had run at which meetings made up transport accounts fairly easily for each owner. After that, having no idea which horses had been shod most, I added all the blacksmith's bills together, divided the total by the number of horses in the yard, and charged the owners a fixed sum for each horse. The training fees would have been easy to calculate if only George had noted when new horses came into the yard and others left, but as no owners complained of being overcharged I suppose their memories were as short as George's.

It was only after I had spent weeks painstakingly writing down each item separately for each owner that I realized that there was not a single bill for veterinary services. Not being able to believe that George's horses were so exceptionally strong and healthy that in six months none of them had needed blistering or to have cuts or coughs attended to, I asked him if he had kept the vet's accounts separately, hoping perhaps to be given a nice tidy little file.

'Bills?' said George. 'Bobby O'Neil has never sent a bill in his life, as far as I know.' And until towards the end of the three years I stayed with George no bill appeared.

Bobby, a happy-go-lucky Irishman, simply could not be bothered to keep accounts either, so between the two of them there was a complete vagueness about the number of Bobby's visits, until in the end Bobby found my continual questions such a nuisance that he too engaged someone to sort things out for him.

When I had at last put everything down into columns I started to add up. The totals were alarming. I was sure I must have made some fundamental mistakes, so as a quick check I added up all George's expenses for the same months and was brought face to face for the first time with the sad truth, that training, like crime, does not pay. George's expenses were slightly more than the money he would receive from the bills I was labouring on.

The loss he had made after all his hard work with the horses did not worry George at all.

'I will put it against the income from the farm,' he said, 'and it will save me a bit of tax.'

It seemed all wrong to me that the job which George took seriously and always put before his farm work should in this way be reduced to the level of an expensive hobby, so I adopted the item called Chemistry, and increased it a little on every bill until the loss disappeared.

'Chemistry' became the symbol of solvency for George from then on, and I have often wondered if any of the owners was surprised at the number of extra pills, drenches, and antiseptics which his horse was apparently needing.

I went to George with the understanding that I would be allowed to ride his horses when the owners did not object to having a beginner on them, but I had not really expected to start very soon. However, I had only been in Cheshire for a week when George said I could ride in a novices steeplechase at Woore a few days later.

'The horse belongs to a friend of mine,' he said, 'and it has never run before.'

As I had never ridden against professional jockeys before, I thought the combination of an untried horse and an untried rider in a novice 'chase on a sharp country course was bound to be a hair-raising affair, but I was thrilled to be given the chance.

'What is it called?' I asked.

'Russian Hero,' said George.

Every morning I had been out with both strings for exercise, galloping and schooling the horses over hurdles and fences, and for the last few days before the race I paid all my attention to the big bay horse I was to ride at Woore. He had, I was told, already run in several point-to-point races, but had had no success, and had fallen once or twice.

When the great day came at last, I followed George into the weighing-room, feeling very strange and a little shy, and was shown to an inconspicuous corner of the changing-room by the valet who was to lend me all my kit. After he had made sure that he had some breeches and a helmet to fit me I went out again to walk round the course.

During my first year or two as a jockey I walked miles, going round every new course I rode on, looking for peculiarities at the jumps and making sure I knew which way to go. It is asking for trouble to go out to race without being certain of the route, and unfair to the man who has asked one to ride for him. One cannot try to gain a few yards by squeezing round a corner if it may turn out to be the wrong one.

I learned this lesson very thoroughly one day at Ludlow a few months later when I was going to ride in a two-horse race for George. I told him, laughing, that I had heard my opponent on the favourite ask somebody where the two-and-a-half-mile starting post was.

George said at once, 'If he doesn't know where the start is, he probably hasn't walked round. You let him go off in front, he may go the wrong way.'

To my surprise, because I had taken George's suggestion

as a joke, that is exactly what happened. When we got near the point where the course separated into the hurdle and steeplechase tracks, I saw the man in front of me waver and hesitate, and he chose the wrong one. He discovered his mistake when he found the wrong sort of fence round the bend, but by the time he got back on to the right course I had a comfortable lead, and I won the race.

I felt so sorry for my opponent when he returned to hear the opinion of the losing half of the crowd, and the more pointed remarks of the horse's owner and trainer, that I promised myself I would always make quite sure of the way before I started.

I did not expect to find myself in front that first day at Woore, but the course was unfenced and, as it was necessary to pass all the marking flags on the outside, it helped to know just where they were.

Back in the weighing-room, changed and weighed out, I sat waiting for the time to go out to the paddock, trying to look calm and unconcerned, as if this was already an everyday affair to me. The summons came at last; George gave me a leg up and some reassuring advice in the parade ring and off I went.

It would be very satisfactory to be able to say that I won that race, but in fact I did not. Russian Hero and I went quietly round together, both of us, perhaps, concentrating on finishing safely without disgracing ourselves, and we came in fourth.

This performance could not have been too hopeless, because after that George asked me to ride quite often, but always, of course, when not much was expected of the horse. Owners had no objection to my riding when their horses were obviously not good enough to win the races they were running in, but they always wanted to put up an experienced jockey if they thought the horse was likely to win. Russian Hero, for instance, had shown so much promise in his first race with me that George decided he was good enough to win a race he was entered for at Birmingham. Jack Bissil rode him, and he won.

Although I understood the owners' feelings very well, I could not help wishing, as time went by, that I could have a chance to win on the horses I had schooled and ridden in their early races. However, I was getting a lot of practice in the art of race riding, even though I rarely finished in the first three. I learned how to judge the pace of a race and to know which of the other horses were going well, how to gain a length by taking an opening on the rails, and how sometimes to avoid trouble by racing on the outside.

Many people were very helpful and gave me good advice. The valets in the weighing-room passed on to me any remarks they had heard about the state of the ground or any changes in the stiffness of the fences.

Jack Moloney, a great cross-country rider, who had been three times second in the Grand National before the war, was still riding when I started and he was exceptionally kind to me. If we were riding in the same race he would never fail to come across to me and tell me something helpful as we were circling round before the start.

'The sun makes bad shadows here in front of the fences,' he said once. 'Don't take off too soon.'

Another time he said, 'Jump the water on the outside. They cut it up badly by the rails in the last race.'

When I was glancing round one day as we lined up he said, 'Don't worry about anyone else. Watch the starter's arm. You'll see his hand press down on the lever which lets the tape up. Jump off then. Don't wait until the tape is actually up.'

I took this advice, and got a flying start in front of the rest of the field. I always tried to do it from then on; but with more caution after the sad day when Joe Murphy set off a second too soon and ran into the tape, which caught in his mouth as it sprang up and pulled four of his teeth out.

Most of the jockeys were not talkative, although they were friendly in their manner. Only one or two of them took an unfair advantage of my inexperience. Once a knee was thrust upwards under my thigh in an attempt to make me lose my balance, and once I was pushed over so far on an

unrailed course that there was no room for me at the jump
and my horse ran out; but these incidents are very un-
common, and there is almost no deliberate rough riding
nowadays.

During the long bitter cold spell of my first winter with
George, he sold his farm and moved his string of horses to
the vast stables near Cholmondeley Castle, where he trained
until 1961. After the move, with its hazards of ferrying all
the horses over roads deep in snow and ice, we settled in
slowly and waited for the thaw.

The season of hunter chases was approaching and I was
hoping that at long last I would be able to win a race. It was
five months then since my first effort on Russian Hero, and
I was getting a little despondent over my lack of success.

The thaw came, racing began again, and the weeks passed
as before. I rode the bad horses, the green horses, and the
tired old horses, but I could not win a race.

The most hopeless mount of all was a wild chestnut who
had got loose one morning and galloped head on into a
signpost. He lost all sense of direction after that.

It was not until the second spring meeting at Bangor-on-
Dee that I broke my duck.

George was running a horse called Wrenbury Tiger in a
hunter chase, and as he thought it would be favourite in the
betting and might easily win, he had engaged Mickey
Moseley to ride it. Mickey, a noted Cheshire horseman, was
hurt a few days before the race, so George asked Dick Black,
who was then a leading amateur, to come instead. Dick
Black said it was too far to come from Berkshire for only one
race and George, not being able to find any other good
amateurs who were free, finally said that I might have a go.

George may have been doubtful of my chances, but I
was delighted at the prospect, and dear Wrenbury Tiger, as
if he knew how much was in the balance for me, behaved
beautifully, made no mistakes, and duly won the race.

Later on that afternoon I was to ride in a novice 'chase
on a horse called Blitz Boy. I had ridden him three or four
times before and we hit the ground every time with depress-

ing regularity. At Bangor-on-Dee my relief and joy at having at last ridden my first winner must have inspired him to greater things, because he cleared all the obstacles with ease, and we won that race too.

It is odd how luck runs. In the few weeks of the season that were left everything went well for me. I won seven more races, which placed me half-way up the amateur jockeys list with the respectable total of nine.

The last day of the season was a rainy one at Newport, Monmouthshire. I was going to ride three good horses, and as Mary was there and we were to be married a week later, I was anxious to end the season with a bang.

I did.

My hopes for the day crashed with me to the ground almost in front of the stands. The horse I was riding got up and galloped straight into the neighbouring river where he swam off strongly downstream, but I stayed painfully where I was, with a snapped collar-bone. And the rain poured endlessly down.

Mary and I were married, the wonderful hot summer wore on, and in August racing began again, in Devonshire.

The Devon circuit is always good fun. It is so far away from home that one must stay down there, and this is an excellent excuse for a few days' holiday by the sea. There is an air of 'back to school' about the first day at Newton Abbot, with everyone greeting the friends they have not seen for a month or two, and gossiping about the pleasures of Majorca or the hardships of water skiing. And some, of course, saying how the rain (or the dry weather) has ruined their hay crop, and that a farmer's lot is not a happy one.

George sent several horses to Devon, to stay there for some weeks and run in the six or seven meetings that are held there every year, and I went down in his place to see that everything went well. It was the first of many such journeys, for I suppose in the years since then I have been to Devon and back about a hundred times.

One of the horses was Rompworthy, a small, compact,

brown gelding which belonged to Mr Dyke Dennis, whose estates Douglas was managing in North Wales. Rompworthy was for two years the mainstay of my existence as a jockey; and Mr Dennis was always very good about letting me ride it instead of asking someone better. Altogether he won thirteen races with me in the saddle, and he was a horse I was very fond of.

He had some odd habits. He preferred left-handed tracks and always went better when it was an advantage for him to jump to the left. He hated being clipped and was so violent that he defeated all attempts, even when a twitch of rope was twisted round his nose. His shaggy and untidy aspect in the winter was no indication of his worth, as many people ruefully learned to their cost when they had backed something else. He was always a most consistent and genuine horse, providing the ground was fairly hard. Only on one surprising day at Chepstow did he ever win in the mud.

Mr Dennis himself was as good to me as his horse. Whenever he was running Rompworthy or one of his other horses at some distance from Cheshire, he would take Mary and me off in his car, with Mrs Dennis, to stay for a day or two near the meeting. We had some hectic and hilarious weekends with him, for he had a great sense of humour and did not care at all what anyone thought of him.

He drove us to Rothbury, one rainy Friday, and when we got there spent hours patiently following all the clues to a black-market ham he had heard of. After two bottles of whisky had loosened the local tongues and a dark and clandestine night journey been made, he returned triumphantly bearing a wizened brown lump as if it were worth its weight in gold. The chase meant far more to him than the ham, for he owned five farms himself and could not have counted his pigs.

The day of Rothbury Races can hardly be said to have dawned, because the sky was dark with rain clouds which almost swamped the hilly little course in the afternoon.

One thin elderly lady must have taken refuge from the cloudburst and had spent her time in the bar absorbing an overdose of alcohol, for, to the utter consternation of all the jockeys, she suddenly appeared at the door of the changing-room, which was a long wooden hut, and asked if this was the way to the ladies' cloakroom. Without waiting for an answer from the stupefied jockeys she ambled calmly down the hut, trailing her wet umbrella behind her, past two rows of open-mouthed men in various stages of undress. She went straight into the washroom at the end of the hut and a little while later walked back and out of the door into the rain again.

No sooner, however, had we stopped laughing than she reappeared in the doorway, walked down the hut into the washroom, and came out again clasping the umbrella.

'I left me gamp,' she said, 'by mistake.'

We did not like to point out that that was not the only mistake she had made, as she still seemed quite unaware of our nakedness.

During my second season with George I rode nearly all his horses regularly, as the owners seemed to be content that I should do so, and I got a tremendous lot of practice. Before the Cheltenham National Hunt Meeting in March, I had ridden in well over a hundred races since the Devonshire circuit, and there were in fact only four professional jockeys who had had more mounts than I.

Russian Hero had won for me at Haydock Park and Leicester, and several of his stable companions had been successful too. One of them, called Salmon Renown, started favourite in a race at Haydock and made a shattering mistake at the second open ditch. He lost a good twenty lengths, but managed not to fall, and we went into the water jump a long way behind the rest of the field. The water jump at Haydock is in front of the stands, and Salmon Renown gave the not-too-pleased crowd another display of acrobatics when he slid almost to a halt on landing. However, on we went, tailed off and almost a fence behind, and disappeared into the haze at the far end of the course. I am told that people on the stands rubbed their eyes and thought we must have taken a short cut, when Salmon Renown and I came back first out of the mist and won comfortably by ten lengths. It was an amazing effort, and it still surprises me, especially as the horse was not very notable afterwards.

I intended to remain an amateur until the end of the season, and was delighted to be asked to ride in most of the important amateur 'chases which all come at that time of the year. The National Hunt Steeplechase, the Foxhunters Chase and the United Hunts Chase at Cheltenham, the Military 'chases at Sandown, and the Foxhunters Chase at Liverpool were among them.

The Stewards of the National Hunt Committee had other ideas. When I arrived at Cheltenham they asked to see me, and in a friendly way pointed out that I was riding so much for no fee that I was possibly taking rides away from professional jockeys who depended on them for their livelihood. Would I either, they said, ride only in amateur races in future, or become a professional and compete fairly for my rides.

I asked to be allowed to go on as before until the end of the season, and at first I thought they would agree, but they changed their minds and decided that I must become a professional at the end of that week.

The thought of missing the Sandown and Liverpool 'chases was very depressing; but as it happened I would not have been able to take part in them in any case, for I broke my collar-bone again on the last day of the Cheltenham meeting, and spent the first three weeks of my professional career with my feet on the ground.

My amateur status had served me very well. I had become known as a rider, and I had been able to partner a lot of horses because I was not allowed to accept any fee. Many of George's owners were farmers, to whom the jockey's, on top of the trainer's, fee was no small matter, and they were glad enough to get someone to ride for nothing. I, in my turn, intending always to be a professional jockey in the end if I should turn out to have any luck at the game, was very pleased to be able to gain so much experience. I looked upon what it cost me to remain an amateur for so long, the travelling expenses, valet's fees, the expensive saddles, breeches and boots, as a sort of capital investment. I was, in effect, buying myself a niche in the professional world.

It was when I won a race for them that the horses' owners found it was embarrassing that I was an amateur. They were forbidden by the rules to give me any reward, or even to pay for my petrol or my train fare, however far I had come to ride for them, and they seemed to think that just saying 'Thank you' was not enough. Quite illegally, there-fore, I was given a small collection of briar pipes, framed photographs, and bottles of wine, which I prized very much, and I ate several celebration dinners as well.

It took me quite a while, after I had become a profes-sional, to shake off a definitely guilty feeling when anyone pressed upon me their thanks in an envelope.

My collar-bone mended again, while I watched the San-down meeting and the Grand National from the stands, and when next I rode the 'Mr' had gone from my name on the number boards. For better or for worse, I had married by licence the life I was leading, and knew that even if I failed completely as a professional I could never ride in amateur races or point-to-points again.

Many people had told me that I would not be offered so many horses when the owners would have to pay me, and that another amateur would be engaged in my place. Luckily for me, however, George's owners had become used to seeing me on their horses and most of them must have decided not to change, for I found I was riding almost as much as before.

The season was nearly over, and George as usual sent several horses up to Cartmel for the Whitsun meeting. I think we all looked forward to Cartmel. We had the greatest fun there, and every Whitsun in the South I wished I could be racing up there instead. We used to stay beside one of the lakes, Grasmere or Windermere or Coniston Water, and motor over for the races.

Hound trails and puppy trails used to be held at Cartmel,

one before and one after the horse races. A man would have run miles over the surrounding hills dragging a bag of aniseed, and shortly afterwards twenty or more hounds were loosed to follow the trail and race each other back. As soon as the returning hounds could be seen in the distance their owners began blowing whistles to encourage them home. It was so funny to see their cheeks swell out with the effort of blowing, and the deep lungfuls of air bursting their chests, because they were making no sound at all. The whistles were all too highly pitched for human ears to hear them, but no one seemed to doubt that the dogs did.

There was tremendous excitement over these hound trails, and the betting was fast and furious. We were told that some keen punters had been known to go up in the hills with a rifle and fire at the favourite as it was streaking away from the field, but no such dastardly skulduggery took place while we were there.

The racing at Cartmel had the same unorthodox air as the hound trails and the fair-ground which crowded upon them. The course is almost round, and all the bookmakers, race-goers, marquees, and the little stands are circled by it. Straight through the middle like a diameter runs the flat stretch to the winning post. It has a rope across it closing it off during the first part of the race, and this is taken away, last time round, for the horses to turn up into the straight for the finish.

On Whit Monday I had been round the mile-long circuit about twelve times and ridden in so many races that I completely lost count in the three-mile hurdle race. I moved up and started to make what I thought was going to be a winning run when I came round the bend and found the rope was still in position. Feeling extremely foolish, I went on round again, but I had upset my mount and we came in second. George, however, forgave me, as I had earlier that day won two races for him and he knew of old how misleading the course could be.

The season was over, it was a wonderfully hot and sunny day, everyone was in high spirits, and all that remained was for us to celebrate these things in a proper manner. The directors of Cartmel invited us to a farewell drink in their square marquee, with their usual hospitality.

I was very happy.

I drank three glasses of excellent champagne on an empty stomach and the whole of Lancashire whirled around me.

FOUR

Black, Gold Sleeves, Red Cap

A telephone call one spring evening in 1948 entirely altered the pleasant routine I had fallen into with George Owen. Harry Bonner, a friend of Father's whom I had known from childhood, rang me up to ask me if I would ride some of Lord Bicester's horses during the next season. Martin Molony was his regular jockey at that time but was often claimed to ride in Ireland, where he lived, and Lord Bicester wanted to retain a second jockey, to be available when Martin was away. Mr Bonner, who was a neighbour and bloodstock adviser to Lord Bicester, suggested me, and so the offer was made.

I could hardly believe my good fortune, and Mary thought I was joking when I told her. It meant that I would be riding the best horses in England, in some of the biggest races, and I was little more than a novice. Lord Bicester's colours carried such prestige on the racecourse that some of it was bound to extend to me, if I did not utterly disgrace them.

George did not hesitate when I asked him what I should do. I did not like to desert him when he had been so kind to me and had given me such a good start.

'You can't possibly refuse that job,' he said, 'it is one of the best there is. Ride Lord Bicester's horses when he wants you, and ride mine in between.'

So it was all settled, the contract was drawn up, and I began an association with Lord Bicester that ended only with his death. I always thought it a great honour to ride for him, and with his passing National Hunt racing lost one of its greatest men.

Lord Bicester's horses did not run in any races during

August or September, so I went down to Devon for George as usual.

Mr and Mrs Dennis drove us down and we stayed in Torquay. The town that summer was full of people and decked with flags and the sea was dotted all over with boats, for the Olympic Games yacht racing was being held there. The Canadian team was staying in our hotel and by the end of the week when someone said, 'What's won?' it was boats and not horses that we were concerned about.

In a week of gaiety and high spirits Mr Dennis contrived to be outstanding. He seemed always to be in the centre of a group of laughing people, and he saw to it that nobody was left feeling lonely. He talked a lot with the Canadians, who were greatly drawn to him. He took us all out in a speed-boat round the moored yachts and kept urging the poor driver to go faster and faster while the spray rose around us in leaping spurts six feet high.

One evening he climbed over the balcony of his room on to the floodlit glass roof which stretched out over the pavement. With him, over the slender metal spars and the brittle glass, he took two intimate articles of bedroom china which he tied on the front of the hotel among the Olympic flags, just over the head of the people passing below. He crawled back to his room, dusted his hands, and happily waited for the storm to break.

A large crowd soon collected on the pavements outside, looking up as if they could hardly believe their eyes. As their numbers grew, they overflowed into the roadway and caused a three-way traffic jam. A slight breeze caused the china objects to clang together every few minutes and the crowd was becoming hysterical.

The manager of the hotel hurried out, gave a horrified gasp, and disappeared again. A policeman came along and looked too, but the long arm of the law could not stretch six feet above his head.

The manager went up to Mr Dennis's room and asked him, as he stood watching with glee the disorganization of Torquay, if he would please go out and recover the hotel's property at once. Mr Dennis, however, pointed out that it was very dangerous to climb out on the flimsy canopy and he did not intend to do it again.

At length the hall porter went out on to the pavement with a pair of steps and, sarcastically encouraged by the enormous crowd, he mounted them and cut down the offending objects. Torquay was gradually restored to normal.

A few weeks later, when Mr Dennis was suddenly dead, we learned that he had known before he went to Devon that he would not live long. Instead of spoiling his own and everyone else's holiday by his gloomy knowledge, he must have been determined, and able, to enjoy to the full the little time he had left.

Some time after our return from Devon, George went down to the Newmarket bloodstock sales and left me in charge of the stables while he was away. I was going round one evening, giving the horses their late feed and seeing that all was well, when I came to Russian Hero's box. Here to my horror I found the pride of the stable grunting with pain, getting down and up again in his box, and sweating a great deal.

Bobby O'Neil arrived at top speed and said Russian Hero had colic. The horse, he said, must not be allowed to lie down. He must be kept walking. So turn and turn about with the lad who usually looked after him, I walked Russian Hero round the yard. The night lengthened, and still we walked. The sky turned grey in the cold dawn and found us trudging on and on, numb and mindless, automatically.

At last the knots in the horse's stomach unwound themselves and he began to walk normally. Wearily we put him back in his box, but there was no time to sleep, for it was almost time to take round the early morning feed.

When George came home he was greatly relieved to find that the horse was quite recovered, because he was looking forward to running him in the Grand National.

In October Lord Bicester's horses came out for their first races of the season. Almost my first appearance in his black, gold, and red colours was on Silver Fame at Worcester. I was thrilled to be sitting on one of the best horses in England, and the race was supposed to be an easy run round for him, for it was certain that he would have no difficulty with the moderate opposition.

We cantered down to the start, and when we got there blood was trickling out of his nose. Silver Fame had obviously broken a small blood vessel.

I did not know what to do.

I did not know if it was usual for the horse to bleed and that it was not serious, or if it had never happened before. Silver Fame's presence at Worcester had been one of the attractions of the meeting, and everyone would be disappointed if he did not run.

Finally, I asked the starter for permission to withdraw, and after looking at the horse's nose and the blood that was still slowly oozing down, he gave it. As I led him back I was still wondering if I was being foolish, but the horse was so valuable that I could not risk harming him.

George Beeby, Lord Bicester's trainer, was hurrying up the course towards me with a worried expression, but when I explained what had happened he said :

'It's a good job you didn't go on. He's never done it before.' And as far as I know he never did it again, although we watched him anxiously for weeks afterwards.

Later on, the same afternoon, I rode Roimond, the second of Lord Bicester's great horses. This time nothing went wrong and to my great relief we won the race.

As George Beeby's training stables were in Berkshire, and George Owen's in Cheshire, I found I was spending a great deal of time driving from one to the other. Often, as the weeks went by, I was in the South when George Owen wanted me in the North, and it became more difficult than we had imagined for me to combine the two jobs. George in the end found it necessary to engage a more regularly available jockey, although I still rode out and did some schooling and his secretarial work for him until I moved to Berkshire eighteen months later. I have always been grateful to George for the start he gave me; we have remained firm friends, and to the end I rode for him occasionally at the northern meetings.

Shortly after the Worcester outings on Silver Fame and Roimond, I rode in my first race at Liverpool. Parthenon, a staid old-fashioned horse of Lord Bicester's, trained by Reg Hobbs, was to run in the Grand Sefton Steeplechase.

Riding for the first time at Liverpool is like crossing the equator : an experience to be looked forward to with awe, a graduation, a widening of horizons. Parthenon, however, was a very safe jumper, so I did not fear an equatorial ducking in Valentine's Brook.

The late Lord Mildmay won the race. It was a great day for him, because he had been trying for years to win a race at Aintree and never done so. Davy Jones ran out with him at the last fence with broken reins when he was almost certain to win the Grand National, and Cromwell had been third in the same race some years later.

Parthenon finished second in the Sefton. He climbed carefully over the large fences all the way round, and as we went over Becher's I had an extensive view of the whole of Liverpool, for what seemed a very long time.

Aintree is a grand racecourse. After two or three fences I began to enjoy my first excursion there, and there was nowhere afterwards that I liked better, as long as I was on a good horse. It is not a place for cowardly horses or bad jumpers, for even the brave and the bold sometimes fall there, and the others would do better to stay at home.

Liverpool is not, as many have heatedly protested, a cruel course. Certainly the fences themselves are larger than anywhere else, and there is a drop to each one on the landing side which is peculiar to Liverpool and at first alarming. It is true that the height and spread of the great open ditch 'Chair' jump in front of the stands are daunting when viewed from the ground, for the fence is taller than a man and three feet wide, the ditch in front is six feet wide, and the guard rail on the take-off side of the ditch is eighteen inches high. No one could say it is an easy course. In addition to the landing drops and the size of the fences, there are several awkward corners, especially after Becher's and at the Canal Turn. Quite often loose horses used to miss the sharp bend to the left there and gallop straight on into the canal, but recently the corner has been fenced.

The two-mile circuit is therefore a testing one, as one might expect from the greatest steeplechase course in the world, but it is also fair. Above all, there is plenty of room. The first five fences are so wide that twenty-five horses could jump them abreast without coming to any harm, and on some country courses there is barely room for six.

People who write indignant letters to newspapers do not realize that Liverpool is a comparatively safe course. Few jockeys are ever badly hurt there, and no more horses die there than anywhere else, although they are given more publicity. If those who strive to have the National course made easier would turn their attentions to improving some of the small courses which really are dangerous in places, there would be more point in them.

The far end of the National course is three-quarters of a mile away from the stands, and it is lonely and silent down there for all races except the National itself. No one is about; there is only the wind, the flying turf, and the long fences. There, everything is simple. The confident stride of a good horse, the soaring lift over the birch, the safe landing, these are the whole of life.

I find I cannot properly describe the ecstasy of Aintree : no one who has not ridden there can understand it, and some of those who have, do not feel it.

Most of the horses which run there positively enjoy Liverpool. Sometimes there have actually been more horses jumping round in the National loose than with jockeys on, even though they could get off the course if they wanted to. Bullingdon, a horse which George Owen trained and which ran in the National in 1948, fell at the first fence; but he got up without his jockey and completed the course of four and a half miles alone. He finished first.

No horse will race properly anywhere if he does not like it. Every rider knows only to well the 'dog' who swishes his tail round like a propeller and makes no effort to quicken his pace when asked to, the soft animal who gives up as soon as he is challenged, the brute who puts his head in the air and sticks his toes in when he does not like the look of a fence. It is simply not economic to run horses which hate racing, for they very rarely win.

There have been qualifying conditions of entry for the National since 1929, when there were sixty-six starters and almost as many casualties. There were a great many runners the year before that also, and only one, Tipperary Tim, finished the course without mishap. It was decided that in future horses must prove their ability before they were acceptable for the great race; they must show they could climb rocks before they attempted Snowdon.

The qualifying rules are simple. Any horse may enter which has :

(a) been placed first, second, third or fourth in any race at Aintree round the Grand National course;

(b) won a steeplechase of three miles or more (of varying qualifying values) during the preceding two years;

(c) won the Maryland Hunt Cup (the amateurs' Grand National) in America.

One can therefore be satisfied that no unwilling horses run in the National, and the people who pity the runners as poor goaded animals with no choice in the matter just do not know the facts.

Parthenon was to have been my first mount in the Grand National, as he had been my first at Liverpool, and Martin Molony was to ride Roimond, Lord Bicester's main hope for the race.

All through the season I had lived for Saturdays, the day that Martin had to be in Ireland. He flew backwards and forwards over the Irish Sea every week, but he was always faithful to Ireland on Saturdays. He was such a brilliant jockey that I could not resent playing second fiddle to him, but I used to long, sometimes, for the air over Dublin to be too turbulent for him to take off.

Martin began his career as a flat-race jockey so he had learned young to ride a hard finish. Also he was a great horseman, and he had such magic in his hands that all horses ran well for him. While I have been racing, there have been few jockeys to compare with him. We were all sorry when, after a very bad fall, he decided not to race any more, but to devote all his time to his farm in Ireland. He still comes over to watch some of the big meetings, and it is always a great pleasure to see him.

In spite of sharing the races with Martin in my first season for Lord Bicester, I had ridden in a good proportion of them, and I was perfectly content to be on Parthenon for my first try at the National.

A few days before the race, however, Martin was hurt in a fall and was not going to be fit enough to ride. There was panic in the Bicester camp. Two horses entered and only one junior jockey, who had never attempted the race before, to ride them.

Lord Bicester himself remained calm. Dick should ride Roimond, he said, and someone else must be found for Parthenon. It was a show of faith in me which I still remember gratefully, and I was determined to do all I could to win for him. He had been trying for nearly thirty years to win the National, but none of his many runners had ever finished nearer than seventh.

The atmosphere in the changing-room on National day is electric.

Suppressed excitement is tightening everyone's muscles, so they do with deliberation and consciously, as if it were all new, the things they do every racing day of the year. Smiles have a different quality : they become an acknowledgement of the hazards ahead, a sympathetic recognition that everyone is suffering from the same tension and the same gripping hope. No one has slept very well, because of this hope. Many have dreamt they have won the race; no one dares to believe that he will.

There are perhaps forty jockeys to be weighed out, so there is a queue by the scales. There is a newsreel camera behind the clerk of the scales, pointing its round eye at you and recording your every blink. Weighed out, you have a last private word with your trainer, who looks as strained as you feel. Then you sit in the changing-room to wait. You have no heart for the chatter and jokes of ordinary days. Rows of silent jockeys sit on the benches, with their elbows on their knees, and stare at their boots. Half an hour passes interminably, until at last, at long last, the time has come.

I thought the nervous excitement I felt before I went out to ride Roimond was because it was my first National, but I felt it every year afterwards. One never gets used to it.

Roimond was looking splendid, his rich dark-chestnut coat gleaming in the March sunlight. As he was carrying top weight and therefore had the lowest number on the race card, we led the parade of horses in numerical order past the stands. I would have been glad to have someone in front of me. It was lonely and awe-inspiring, walking up the course under the gaze of a quarter of a million people.

Once we were off, however, there was no time for emotion. Choose the opening, present the horse, jump the fence, think forward to the next one.

Roimond made no serious mistakes as we went twice round the long circuit. He was leading for some of the way, and was always going well in the first five or six. As we started the last mile he was so easily holding his own against all the other horses I could see that I began to think that, incredibly, I might actually be going to win. The next moment, however, two horses came past me, and one was going so fast that I knew I could not overtake him again. Roimond jumped the last fence in third place, but struggled up into second as we raced towards the winning post.

Ahead of me, flashing away, I could see the familiar black-and-white quartered colours, the very jersey I had worn so often myself, of the winner, Russian Hero.

Lord Bicester was delighted to be as near as second. He comfortingly said that the great difference in the weight they were carrying had been the cause of Russian Hero's beating his horse. But nothing he could say could take away the irony of the situation. Russian Hero had won; the horse I had ridden to victory so often myself, the horse whose life I had possibly saved when he had colic, the horse, moreover, who had fallen in his last three races before the National and who was known to jump well only if he met the fence correctly.

George Owen had even been doubtful of running him at all. He had wanted to run him in an easier race earlier in the week, but his owner, Fearnie Williamson, insisted on his taking his chance in the National.

In spite of my personal disappointment, I could not help being glad for George's sake that he had trained the National winner. Always a quiet man, he was absolutely speechless with pleasure, and his broad smile seemed like a permanent fixture on his happy face.

In the weighing-room the tension had dissolved. Champagne corks were popping, backs were being slapped, betting tales as improbable as fishing stories were being swapped, and a hundred voices were raised in excited discussion.

It is the same every year.

Before the war, when the National was run on Friday and everyone was staying for the Saturday races, the winning owner gave a party in Liverpool on Friday night. Since the war, however, the National is usually held on a Saturday, and at the end of the day nearly everyone goes home, so the party, which is sometimes not given that night at all, is only a shadow of its former glory.

Fearnie Williamson's party was different. He is a prosperous Cheshire farmer and he wanted to have a Cheshire party.

A hotel in Chester astonishingly agreed to put on a dinner for about a hundred people at fours hours' notice and the great win was properly celebrated. Everyone made speeches. Fearnie made a speech. George made a speech. Leo McMorrow, who rode the horse, made a speech. I said that if I had known Russian Hero would beat me in the National I would certainly have let him die of colic, but there was no one I would have wanted to win more than George, if I

could not. George, Fearnie and Leo said there was no one
they would rather see win than me, if they had not.

It got a little complicated and misty-eyed towards the
end, but it was a great evening.

The cause of it all, the Hero of the occasion, was munching his ordinary feed back in his own quiet stable. He did
not know he was famous.

After Liverpool the rest of the season goes on for two months,
during which the three lesser 'Nationals' take place – the
Scots, the Irish, and the Welsh. The meetings get fewer
every week, the one-day country meetings are held, and the
big courses gradually change over to flat racing. The last
steeplechase meeting at Chepstow is at Easter, when the
Welsh National is run.

One morning after Russian Hero's National I was up on
the Berkshire Downs, schooling some of Lord Bicester's
horses for George Beeby, when he asked me to school a
horse for Ken Cundell. I had not met Ken before. He lived
in Compton, the same village as George Beeby, and he had
been training on his own for only a few seasons.

Ken gave me a leg up on to a compact chestnut with a
very white face and four white socks, and I took the horse
up over George Beeby's excellent schooling fences. He was
a wonderful jumper. Ken explained that his usual jockey
had gone home to Ireland, and asked me if I would ride the
chestnut at Cheltenham a few days later. I was glad to. The
race was a novice 'chase and Hereford, the chestnut, had
never run over fences before, although he had won hurdle
races. He took to Cheltenham like a veteran, led all the way
round, flew over the fences, and won easily.

Ken asked me on the spot to ride for him in the Welsh
National, and his entry, Fighting Line, won that easily too.

It was some compensation to me, after being second on
Roimond; and by a strange coincidence the only other time
I won the Welsh National was just after Devon Loch had
come so close to winning the big race. Lose one, and win
the other, has been the pattern for me twice.

About the time that I started riding for Ken, Gerald Balding asked me to ride some of his horses too, and it was settled that when Lord Bicester did not need me I would, during the next season, ride for him, and for Ken as well.

I was now to ride regularly for three stables which were all in the south of England, and we still lived in Cheshire. The continual journeys backwards and forwards were tiresome, but there seemed to be no houses to let near Compton and Mary and I were very fond of our flat in Cheshire. The flat was a converted hayloft, and we had spent much time and energy in painting every inch of it and making it into a comfortable home.

The dilemma was solved for us in an unpleasant way.

One morning in October Mary and I parted for a week. She was going to London to stay with her mother and I was to ride in Scotland, at Kelso, and then spend a night with my uncle at Cheltenham, over the Chepstow meeting a few days later. I rang Mary up once or twice during the week and she said she had influenza and was feeling a little weak, but neither of us thought anything of it as we both have strong constitutions.

Then one morning, as my uncle and I were preparing to leave his house on our way to Chepstow races, the telephone rang. It was Mary.

She said, 'Darling, you are not to worry, but I shall not be here when you come to London this evening. I have got to go to hospital.'

She sounded quite light-hearted.

'What is the matter with you?' I asked. I almost thought she was joking.

She said, 'It is really only a formality, but I have got a notifiable illness and there is no choice about it. I have got to go to an isolation hospital.'

'Is it measles,' I asked, 'or perhaps scarlet fever?'

'No,' she said. 'As a matter of fact – and you are not to worry because I am quite all right – as a matter of fact it is infantile paralysis.'

We talked some more, and she was laughing. I asked if she would like me to come up to London instead of going to Chepstow, but she would not hear of it.

'I am quite all right. Come and see me this evening,' she said.

I drove up to London fast after the races and out to Neasden Isolation Hospital.

Mary had certainly sounded all right, as she had said, on the telephone. But she did not look all right. Her face was yellow and grey, and she looked ill and old. It was clear that she was very far from being all right.

The following evening she was moved into an artificial respirator. I had promised my parents I would let them know how she was, so I walked out to the telephone kiosk at the hospital gates. As I dialled the number my mind was filled with the image of Mary as I had just left her, with only her head free of the grey-painted wooden box which enclosed her body while a big electric bellows pumped air in and out of her lungs. I stood trembling and shaking with the receiver in my hand, and when Mother answered and I tried to speak to her I found I was uncontrollably crying.

I hated having to leave Mary alone and go on racing, but the doctors assured me that her life was not in immediate danger and she herself insisted, as usual, that she was 'quite all right'. So every day, after I had ridden, I drove back to Neasden.

It was a wonderful hospital, and no praise is too high. There were no visiting hours, for visits to polio patients were not restricted at all. One Saturday I drove down from Liverpool after racing there and did not arrive until half-past nine in the evening; the night sister not only seemed glad to see me but she gave me some supper as well.

At Wolverhampton one day I had a fall, but felt nothing wrong, and drove off as usual towards London. When the warmth died out of me in the November air, and my muscles stiffened, I found I could not move my left arm properly. I was through the outskirts of Wolverhampton and wondered whether I should turn back for some treatment, but

decided it would be better to go on because I was bound for
a hospital in any case.

After a short while I could not put my hand back on to
the gear-lever to change gear. I stopped the car, put my left
hand on to the gear-lever knob with my right hand, and
started off again. Luckily it was a car with a short lever
rising from the floor close to my left side, so that the force
of gravity was helping to hold my hand on it. I drove all the
way from Wolverhampton to London without taking my
hand off the gear lever, trying to convince myself that my
forearm muscles were only bruised, and that no bones were
broken.

There were some good horses for me to ride at the Manchester November meeting at the end of the week, and at
Birmingham and Cheltenham after that, so I spent the next
two days, which were free, with Mary, anxiously wiggling
my fingers to see if they were still in working order.

A dozen races and two winners later, I broke my collar-
bone again at Cheltenham and went to London to have it
dealt with by Bill Tucker. When my shoulder was strapped
up, I asked him if I could have some massage on my left
arm. He felt it, and I could see his fingers stop as they came
to the bump I had been trying to persuade myself was not
there.

'You've broken it,' he said accusingly, 'and you must
have known. One bone in your forearm has been acting as a
splint for the other.'

He made me a removable plaster cast to wear, and for
the next fortnight I sat with Mary doing crossword puzzles
while the cracks quietly knitted together again.

Bill Tucker is an institution that many of us could not
do without. He is that rare man, a surgeon who realizes that
if muscles are allowed to rest while bones mend, the total
recovery time will be prolonged. From the first he prescribes
gentle massage and faradism, an electric treatment which
exercises muscles while the owner of them relaxes and thinks
about something else.

Mr Tucker's special interest is in injuries to people whose

livelihood depends on their being fit. Ballet dancers, cricketers, and rugger players, as well as jockeys, are among his regular patients, and he patches them up and sends them back to their jobs as fast as he can.

While Mary was in hospital Ken Cundell asked me if I was still looking for a house in Berkshire. I said that indeed I was, but had had very little time to see about it lately. He then offered me the house he had once lived in himself, which was empty. I was very pleased by the suggestion and delighted when I saw the house. It is a very old black-and-white-fronted house with many small tiled gables, settling into the ground as old houses do.

Ken showed me round it, and apologized that one entire outside wall was missing; it was being rebuilt. There were several other repairs to be done and the whole of the inside was to be decorated, so the house would not be ready to live in until the following March.

Mary and I were both glad that the uncertainty about where we were to live had ended so pleasantly, and she spent many hours, before she left hospital, mentally arranging furniture in rooms she had never seen.

During the months before the house was ready for us we lived in London, for after she had left hospital Mary still had to go every day for treatment for her weak muscles. We never lived again in our first home, the hayloft flat.

In March the move to Compton was completed. A week or two later I left Mary in Oxford and went up to ride at Bangor-on-Dee races.

Bangor-on-Dee has always been a course of good omen for me. It was there that I rode in my first race under National Hunt rules; it was there that I rode my first winner; and it was there that I first rode three winners in one afternoon. So it was not really surprising that it should have been on the day of Bangor-on-Dee races that our first son was born. I drove down in record time from Bangor, and arrived in Oxford half an hour before he did.

FIVE

It's an Up and Down Life

By the autumn of 1950, when the new season began, life had arranged things very happily and tidily for us. Mary was gaining strength every day and her hands and wrists, which had been badly affected, were gradually beginning to work again. Our small son was thriving, we were settled into our pleasant house, and I was riding for two stables which were both in the same village. Some of Ken Cundell's horses, in fact, were stabled opposite our kitchen windows, so my work was literally on the doorstep.

The season before had been a very lonely one for Mary and me. I had had to leave her sometimes for days at a time, and it was a great joy and relief to both of us when she was strong enough, a year after she became ill, to come with me again on my travels.

In all the years she has been going to meetings with me, Mary's interest in racing has remained mild, though she knows a good deal about it by now. She is no longer liable to repeat the answer she gave someone years ago who asked what colour Roimond was.

'Auburn,' she said.

The reaction of the racing fraternity to this remark was worthy of a Bateman drawing.

Before we met, Mary had never been to a race meeting, but after our marriage she went with me every day she possibly could, to keep me company and, as she callously said, 'to pick up the bits'. Mary used to ride as a child, but no longer feels any urge to do so. She never studies the form book, never has a bet, and we hardly ever talk about horses at home : a most restful state of affairs for us both.

During our engagement several members of our families

gloomily foretold that Mary's lack of interest in horses would be the downfall of our marriage, but from the first it was a joke between us, and through the years we have found it has balanced my own single-minded concentration into a shared sense of proportion.

It cannot be easy to be a jockey's wife, or indeed to be the wife of any sportsman whose sole aim is to go faster than the rivals on his heels. Day after day she may wait on the stands, anxiously watching her husband take the unavoidable risks of his profession, happily cheering him home when he wins, but knowing for a certainty that sooner or later the bad falls will come, like kings disastrously turning up in a game of clock patience.

Nearly everyone used to ask Mary the same question :

'Don't you worry when your husband is racing?'

And I have heard her answer, with a comic expression of self-mockery :

'Only when they start waving the white flag for the ambulance.'

But Mary tells me that all jockeys' wives, however united a front of composure they show to the world, and however lightly they evade the truthful answer, find a familiar dread lying in wait for them every time the tapes go up, and the thousandth time is as bad as the first.

I also was often asked if I ever felt any qualms for my own safety, and I said honestly that I did not, for I never expected to fall and I sometimes found it hard to believe that all was lost, even when my close contact with the ground was a depressing reality.

However, it might be as well to get the whole business of injuries into some sort of perspective, as it is his body's growing loss of resilience which forces every steeplechase jockey, near his fortieth birthday, into a retirement for which his heart and mind may be unready.

I suppose that on an average during a whole season one may expect to fall about once in fifteen races, though the proportion may be a good deal lower than that for a jockey who only rides in hurdle races.

The usual course of events, when one has ruefully picked oneself up and inspected for indecency the torn breeches which are going to cost more to replace than the fee one was paid for wearing them, is to totter off on the long tramp back to the weighing-room. All jockeys complain that their mounts unerringly part company with them, as if by instinct, at the farthest point from home, and although it is of course possible to lie still and feign rigor mortis until the ambulance comes dashing up to collect the corpse, this sensible way of securing a lift back is apt to be unpopular with one's beloved on the stands.

One extremely wet day at Southwell, however, I warned Mary that if I should fall at the far end of the course she could be almost sure that any white-flag-waving would only be the result of some realistic play-acting on my part, as I had no intention of walking half a mile in the mud in my thin racing boots if it could be avoided. To my disgust, the horse I was riding slid ten yards on his haunches as he landed over the farthest hurdle and threw me off on to the squelching turf.

All according to plan I rubbed at an uninjured ankle until the nearest first-aid man held up his sodden white flag and waved it about in the rain. The ambulance trundled slowly up the field towards me and stopped about a hundred yards away. My first-aider walked off to find out why he had not come any nearer and came back to tell me that the driver said the ground was too wet, and the ambulance would be driving into a bog if he came any farther. Would I, he asked, try to get to the ambulance with his help, in spite of my no doubt grave injuries. I rose at once, and we walked towards the waiting van, but most unfortunately I forgot to limp and before we reached it the ambulance suddenly backed away, turned round, and drove implacably off back to the stands without me. As I slithered and slid my cold way down the course, soaked to the skin and with every prospect of being late for my next race, I cursed the black heart of that unfriendly ambulance·driver with every unprintable oath I could think of.

The standard of efficiency, good-humour and common sense among first-aid men at race meetings varies wildly from the unsurpassably good to the frankly terrifying. To those of them who know their job one cannot be too grateful, for they stand for hours in the wind and rain, in lonely places beside the scattered fences, on the chance that someone will fall there and need their help. But the bad ones are a menace to life and especially limb. I did not believe it when I was told that one first-aider had picked up my wrists, and another my ankles, and between them had lifted and swung my unconscious body off the course in this fashion, until a few weeks later, when I saw the same thing happen to Fred Winter at the same fence. If either of us had had a broken or dislocated arm or leg or spine, we would have suffered far more damage from the 'first-aid' than from the fall itself. A broken bone could have ripped its way through muscle and skin, nerves, ligaments or spinal cord could have been irreparably torn, and we in our helpless unconsciousness could not have felt the pain that would have forced our rescuers to be careful if we had been awake.

After a fall, whether he has returned on his horse, on foot, or in the 'blood wagon', every jockey must be passed fit by a doctor before he may ride again, so a detour to the first-aid room is routine.

One goes in, says to the doctor, 'I had a fall, but there's no damage,' and if one is obviously in a healthy state he nods his agreement and one is free to go off and repeat the whole dreary business. One afternoon I fell three times without harm, and the third time I appeared the doctor laughed at me and said, 'Why don't you just wait here until after the next race? It will be so much less trouble for you than bothering to start off on a horse and walking back.'

The morning after a fall one may wake up stiff and during the day discover that sundry small areas of skin are missing, or notice a large bruise on some part that one cannot even remember bumping, but that is all the trouble one should expect from the majority of falls.

Really bad falls are mercifully rare, and some of the most

appalling-looking crashes leave both jockey and horse un-hurt. One day at Sandown Park, Fighting Line fell with me and rolled right over me but, incredible as it may seem from the series of photographs which was taken of this catastrophe, I was hardly even bruised. At Towcester I fell on my head over the last fence and was knocked out, and I was told that the horse I was riding lay winded on top of my head and shoulders so that for some minutes all that could be seen of me was an inert pair of legs. The horse rocked backwards and forwards on me as he struggled to his feet, but an hour later I was driving home, without so much as a headache.

There is about one chance in five hundred of being killed : that is to say, of roughly five hundred jockeys riding, an average of one is killed every year. The chances of being badly hurt for a long time, or for life, are only slightly higher. Fred Winter broke his back one year, and his leg another, and missed a whole season each time. George Slack broke his shoulder when schooling one morning in January 1956 and he lost nearly two years. Lionel Vick severed his spinal cord high up in his back and became an incorporated accountant in his wheel chair. A fractured skull ended the riding careers of George Owen, Martin Molony and Fred Thackeray. Fred Rimell rode in a race for the last time on the day he should have been the guest of honour at the dinner given to celebrate his being Champion Jockey. He spent the evening in Cheltenham Hospital instead, with a broken neck.

The tale of woe goes back to the beginning of steeple-chasing.

The number of bones each jockey may expect to break varies a great deal, because some men have strong bones, and others brittle. Jack Dowdeswell's collar-bones broke so often and so easily that in the end he had them taken out. On the other hand, Tim Molony was made of india-rubber. He had his share of falls, but the only big bone I recall his breaking was his leg, which finished his career in 1958. One or two of mine cracked every season. My nose and ribs are no longer in mint condition and my collar-bone score to date is twelve.

Most injuries are to shoulders, because that is usually the part which meets the ground first. The best way to fall is to roll as soon as the shoulder touches the ground, tuck in the head, draw the knees up and stay still, for it is much easier for a horse galloping over a man to avoid kicking him if he is not moving. Some of the very worst injuries are due to being kicked when one is still rolling from a fall, but horses will avoid fallen riders if they possibly can. It is extremely stupid and very dangerous to try to get up before all the horses have gone safely past.

If you fall on your head you are not likely to know about it for some time. The thin cotton and shellac wall of a crash helmet saves your life, but probably ruins itself doing so, and a trek to London for a new one becomes an urgent errand. Races are run at an average speed of thirty miles an hour and falling on the unprotected head at that pace may well be final. It is interesting that since September 1956 all flat-race jockeys have also been compelled by regulations to wear crash helmets because, although they are not often pitched off on to their heads, there have been times for them too when a helmet could have diminished bad concussion to a bump.

Although it may seem that steeplechase jockeys are reck-lessly risking their lives in a dangerous sport, it is a matter of record that the death rate of window cleaners is very much higher. If any window cleaners' wives are reading this, I sincerely apologize for passing on this most unwel-come piece of news.

I would be interested to know whether insurance com-panies accept the custom of window cleaners, for very few of them will take on a National Hunt jockey except at a premium so large that he would have to be hurt for two months before the company had even paid back to him his own money. When I was an amateur I tried several insurance companies and was finally allowed to pay one of the biggest of them a large sum of money each year, which was to be returned to me in small instalments if I should be injured; and to my amusement and mystification, the policy said I was to be paid double in the melancholy event of my losing an arm or leg on the railway.

After three years the company would not renew their agreement with me, in spite of having made a good profit from my excellent health. I am very grateful to them, for if I had gone on paying the premium their profit by now would be so enormous that I would have to lie in front of a train if they were to lose money on the deal.

Luckily, however, there is a comforting institution called the Levy Board Accident Scheme which pays a weekly sum to any jockey who is unable to ride because he has been injured. Into this fund every jockey pays a small proportion of every riding fee he receives.

It is an ironic fact that when I rode in enough races I usually paid to the injury fund more than I did to the insurance company; but at least I had the pleasure of knowing I was helping my investments to get back into the saddle as quickly as possible.

The enemy which puts more jockeys out of work than any injury is the weather : and if anyone should think that their anxiety to switch on any nearby wireless when the warnings of the meteorological office are due on the air is in any way obsessive, he probably does not know that bad weather not only often keeps them grounded but also upsets the form of the horses they ride, so that they find perhaps that a horse they were looking forward to winning on when the ground was hard is skidding and hopeless after rain has made the surface slippery.

The steeplechasing season begins on the first of August and ends on the following Whit Monday but is at its height only from October until the Grand National at the end of March, and every winter we waste days and weeks of these precious six months staring out of the window at the frozen ground and wishing we could shift the British Isles ten degrees south.

In the year 1955 racing was abandoned for the following reasons: snow, frost, fog, waterlogged ground, and large cracks due to drought. Worcester racecourse was flooded to a depth of five feet by the overflowing Severn, and Newton Abbot was ruined for a year by sea water from a breached canal.

Fog is the most annoying thing of all. Frost and floods are at least definite, and the impersonal voice of the 9 AM newsreader saves many a useless journey, but fog is so mobile and so local that racing is not usually abandoned because of it until the scheduled time for the first race is drawing near. So off one goes in the mist, starting an hour earlier than usual, and drives perhaps a hundred miles to discover whether one can see the last hurdle and the last fence from the stands. If these obstacles remain infuriatingly out of sight, back one creeps in the murk and the gloom and arrives home very tired, with fog-strained eyes, lungs, and temper.

One can never be sure that at the last moment racing will be possible after all, for fog is freakish stuff. One November day, when fog had been accurately forecast to smother the Midlands, we slowly drove into Wolverhampton, where at noon the streets were indistinct in a yellowish-black oily cloud, to the racecourse beside the railway lines two or three hundred yards farther on. To our utter astonishment and delight the mist there was thin and white, and all the races were held without question and at the right times. At the end of the afternoon we drove out of the car park straight back into the night that had lasted all day in Wolverhampton.

When I arrived one morning at Sandown Park and walked up to the weighing-room in the bright April sunshine, I was surprised by the lack of the usual bustle there.

'It's the fog,' said the valets.

'Fog?' I looked rather wildly out of the window at the blue sky.

'Go and look at the course,' they said.

So I walked down the slope from the weighing-room with the sun warm on my back and through the archway under the stands to the course. I could see nothing, and it was cold. The swirling mist had collected on the lower ground and had banked up against the long line of massive stands, and although it looked so light and fluffy there it stayed while we cursed it in the sunshine ten yards away, and there we left it an hour later when we all went home.

Hailstorms, bitter winds, and fog with about two hundred yards visibility do not interfere with the racing programme itself, although a jockey may find it somewhat difficult to ride a clever and well-judged race if he can hardly see where he is going; and the crowds are mostly concerned with avoiding frostbite between races in the bars. However, not even the rigours of our officially temperate climate can cool the true devotee's enthusiasm for the sport to the point of keeping him at home so that even in the worst of raceable weather there are still to be seen the mournfully dripping groups of punters under the bookmakers' umbrellas, the stable lads, blue-nosed and red-fingered in the cold stolidly trudging round and round the parade ring with their horses, and the shapeless mackintoshed bundles in sheepskin boots and head-scarves hurrying to put fifty pence each way from the housekeeping money on the Tote.

Only once was I actually overtaken by a blizzard. I had been engaged to ride Gallery in the National Trial Steeplechase at Wetherby, and Mary and I set off to go there across country by train as the car was having its appendix out, or some such operation on its broken-down interior.

Everything that the railways could do had been done to make that journey the most spectacularly uncomfortable one we had ever undergone, not excluding the day we crossed the bleak black-rock Pennines in a freezing wind in a borrowed open two-seater MG and had a puncture in the snow at the top.

As I went out on Gallery for the fourth race a few snowflakes were beginning to fall, and as we circled round at the starting gate they swirled about us thicker and thicker, until they enclosed us completely and we could no longer see the stands or the fences. For a quarter of an hour we walked round in a circle while the snow fell steadily into our eyes and down our necks and settled quickly on the ground.

When it became so deep that even if it stopped at once there was more than enough to ball up in the horses' feet and prevent them galloping properly, the race was abandoned, and we rode disconsolately back to the paddock looking like a row of mounted snowmen.

Back to Cheshire went Mary and I on the long succession of chilly buses and trains, noticing that the coal fires in the waiting-rooms of both the Manchester stations seemed to consist of the identical black and faintly smoking lumps we had huddled over in the morning.

There was only one consolation for our pointless journey, and that was that in spite of the fact of their not having started the race all the jockeys were to be paid their fees as if they had. Not long before this a fee was only paid if the horse and its rider actually came under starter's orders, but after one or two incidents when jockeys had been thrown and hurt in the paddock or on their way to the start, or their mounts had injured themselves and had been withdrawn at the post, it was decided that a fee was owing to a jockey as soon as he had passed the scales.

The new ruling could not have found a better justification than the blizzard race at Wetherby, but as the full beauty of it slowly dawned upon the ranks of jockeys some curious things happened. Several Clerks of the Scales, for instance, could not account for the eagerness of a queue of grinning jockeys who had changed into racing colours much earlier than usual to pass out for the first race on foggy days, when it was probable that they would immediately have to get dressed again and go home. One or two enterprising young criminals worked out a scheme for passing the scales (and so being paid a fee) for riding a horse which had not even been declared a runner for the race; but their ingenious plotting was never put to the test. The Clerks of the Scales were all at once deeply suspicious of every jockey weighing out a minute before it was necessary, and on misty days horses, trainers and owners had almost to be waiting in the paddock before their jockeys were allowed to pass the money barrier of the weighing machine. Alas, the fun went out of the game, but the rule itself proved its value and after several years of fair application and no abuse has faded into one of the things we gratefully take for granted.

The discomfort one brings upon oneself from injury and bitter weather is often enough to make one wonder aloud, 'Why on earth be a jockey?' but before I can try to answer that question there is another disadvantage to be considered, a disadvantage less physical and less definite than the other two, but perhaps more painful all the same. This, simply, is disappointment.

There is first the direct disappointment of missing races through injury or frost, and this is an uncomplicated emotion because one knows one cannot alter the weather, or ride if one is unfit. The bones will mend, the thaw will come, and all will be well again.

Secondly, there is the disappointment of losing a race one had reasonably hoped to win, and the heavy feeling of knowing that all the trainer's hard work has been wasted and the owner's hopes been extinguished. The most usual cause of this common frustration is that another horse has proved better on the day, for however eager or skilful the jockey may be, and however great his will to win, he cannot succeed if his mount is not good enough.

So many things can go wrong which no jockey can foresee or avoid, and three seconds delay, for any reason, is enough to lose most races. One's horse may not be feeling on top of the world at the right moment, he may not like the hardness, softness or slipperiness of the ground, he may hit a fence a bit hard and jump too cautiously from then on, he may be baulked or knocked over by other horses who are themselves unbalanced or falling, or he may tangle his legs up and fall himself, in spite of all his jockey's efforts to get him to meet a fence well. The horse may injure himself by pulling a tendon, or by striking into his forelegs with his hind feet, or by staking himself in a losing argument with a hurdle, and have to drop out of the race.

One may even pass the winning post first and then lose the race on an objection from the second, perhaps because one's horse was too tired to keep a straight course and crossed or pushed over the line behind; or perhaps on the technicality that one's mount was not qualified for the race, or was carrying the wrong weight. There is little that is more dispiriting to a jockey than to find that his hard-ridden and hard-won race has been taken away from him and awarded to someone else. Until 1955, a horse disqualified from winning was automatically placed last, but the modern rule is more merciful, and where it is clear it was from accident and not malice that one horse prevented another from winning the Stewards may simply reverse the placing of the two horses concerned.

Then there are the saddles which slip backwards and swing under the horse's belly on loose girths, the reins and stirrup leathers which break, and the bits which come apart beside the horse's mouth.

One day at Warwick I rode a horse called Quick One for George Owen. There were very few runners in the race because Four Ten, the Gold Cup winner, was certain to win it unless he fell, and George asked me to lie just behind Four Ten all the way in case the unexpected should happen. George was slightly disconcerted when he saw his horse shoot to the front after the first fence, with his jockey apparently disregarding all the agreed plans : but not nearly as disconcerted as the jockey himself. As Quick One landed over the first fence his bit broke and fell out of his mouth, so that for the whole three miles of the race I was a helpless passenger. Luckily the course was railed all the way round, and Quick One showed no desire to run out, so on we went with the horse in full control of the situation and me sitting on top without brakes or steering.

Four Ten passed us effortlessly between the last two fences and Quick One finished second. I could not pull up and I had visions of my tireless mount going round the course yet again, but he took a hint from Four Ten slowing down in front of us and followed him faithfully back to the paddock. George apologized for the calamity, explaining that the metal must have been faulty, as the bridle was new.

As George had not expected his horse to win, the whole performance was extraordinarily comic, but it would have been a very sad affair if it had happened when months of planning and hard work had been devoted to the winning of a particular race.

The failure of part of the harness is apt to be drastic when it occurs, but it is not a usual cause of the abrupt dissolving of the partnership between horse and jockey. It is only too easy to fall off when one's mount stumbles over a fence or hurdle, or stops to take an extra stride before he jumps, or pecks and puts his head down on landing, but it does not lessen one's disappointment as one trudges earthbound back to the paddock, to meet the equally downcast faces of owners and trainers.

These falls are among the third sort of disappointments, those which are hardest to bear because there is always the uncomfortable suspicion that they are one's own fault; and the races that might have been won by different tactics are the most difficult to forget. There is the dilemma of the risky opening : taken with success it can lead to acclaim as a useful bit of riding; taken with disastrous results it leaves one cursing one's folly in attempting it.

Sometimes one misjudges the pace of a race and makes a winning effort too soon or too late, so that one's horse is not in front at the essential moment. There is not an honest jockey riding who will not admit to having been disappointed in himself for a depressing mistake now and then.

Finally there are the bitter times when an owner or trainer decides that he wants to change his jockey. I do of course understand that the winning of races is the whole point of owning and training racehorses, and that it is only common sense to engage the jockey most suited to the type of horse and race, so that the horse shall have the best possible chance. If a jockey has made an obvious mess of a race

he may learn with regret, but not with surprise, that someone else has been engaged for the horse's next attempt; or
an owner may well feel that he has a better chance in a
hurdle race with jockey A than with jockey B, or that
jockey C can ride a strong-pulling horse better than jockey
D, and may choose his man accordingly. Nevertheless there
are few jockeys who do not feel that at one time or another
they have lost rides, or even a job with a stable, for no
reason at all. From what I have heard from others and felt
myself, it is the seeming injustice of these blows which hurts
more than the actual loss of the riding.

Last spring I stood beside a friend on the stands while
we watched a horse he had often ridden win a race.

'Why aren't you riding it?' I asked.

'I don't know,' he said in a defeated voice, 'I just don't
know. I have won nine races on that horse for his owner,
and now he has put someone else up. He didn't tell me why.
What more can you do than win?'

He spoke for all of us who have ever felt ourselves in the
same position.

At the other end of the scale is the moment of fulfilment
when there is no one ahead on the ribbon of grass stretching away between the shouting crowds and one goes past
the winning post first.

Sometimes a horse proves so much better than anyone
has thought him that it is a great surprise when he wins,
but usually hours of effort and planning are behind the
happy ending in the winner's unsaddling enclosure. From
the day a horse joins a trainer's stable everyone's aim is to
bring him to his lean peak of fitness, to teach him to jump
cleanly, to feed and groom him until his coat is shining
with health, and to care for his feet and legs so that these,
the weakest parts of a horse's anatomy, will not fail him
when he relies on their strength as he lands over a fence or
thrusts himself forward to win with all the power of his
massive hind-quarters.

When a jockey trots out to ride a race he takes to his task
not only his own skill but all the hard work of trainer, stable-

lad and blacksmith as well, and when the horse wins it is a
reward shared by them all. As well as my own simple
pleasure in winning, the last stride past the post brought to
me freshly every time a feeling of relief that the efforts of all
these people had not been wasted. Their delight was my
satisfaction, the owner's joy was my reward, all was right
with the world, and I knew why on earth I was a jockey.

Surely anyone is a happy man who can spend his life
doing what he likes best, and make a career of it too. Being
a jockey is more than a job, it is a way of living. It is the
way I liked to live; and although I no longer ride in races,
my interest, my heart, and my work take me almost as much
as ever to a racecourse.

By nature I am a restless man, and I hate to stay long
in one place. For two months in the summer every year
there is no steeplechasing and this long break, which seemed
in the depths of winter to beckon like a soft bed to a tired
body, soon palled for me. After a fortnight's rest I wanted
to start racing again, but every year I had to summon what
patience I could to bear the banishment until August.

In the early summer Mary and I often go for a quiet
holiday on our own, perhaps driving round Scotland or
Europe in a car, or round the Norfolk rivers in a boat, but
always moving on, so that there is something new to see
every day and a new place to remember. We drift where
we like and when, without planning in advance or fussing
over time-tables, and with no one to consult but ourselves.
This lazy and aimless touring is rest and refreshment for us
both, but holidays which mean only lying on the sand in the
sun bore me hopelessly. I always feel, as soon as I am idly
stretched out, that I must be up and doing something or
going somewhere, even if it is only for a game of tennis or a
walk with the children along the beach to the toffee-apple
stall.

It is therefore not surprising that I actually enjoy the
daily travelling to race meetings and, unless it is misty or
the roads are choked with traffic, I very rarely find any
journey tedious. Unfortunately the traffic problem affects

us a great deal as we are always in the middle of it on Saturdays and Bank Holidays; needless to say, we are going where the crowds are. The queues of cars to Liverpool, Cheltenham, Plumpton, Wolverhampton and Bangor-on-Dee have sometimes been so long and snail-like that there is often to be seen a dismal march along the road of the jockeys engaged for the first race who know it is quicker on foot.

When I started racing in 1946 the war-time petrol rationing for cars was still very strict, and I went quite thoroughly into the idea of buying an aeroplane to go racing in, because it was then easy and cheap to buy an Auster and petrol for flying was unrationed. Flat-race jockeys regularly fly to meetings and aircraft landing on steeplechase courses are not unknown, but two things defeated my hopeful plans.

First and worse was the weather, for there are too many days when racing is possible but flying is not. Gale-force winds, very low cloud, poor visibility and rain storms would keep me grounded, and a great many of the journeys home would have to be made in the early winter darkness.

Secondly, there were a tremendous number of regulations pressing down the would-be private flyer. One was not allowed to park one's plane in the back garden and take off at a moment's notice, or to land anywhere without permission in triplicate or a blind eye.

I found I would have to leave the plane at the nearest civilian airport and drive over there when I wanted to use it. Also I would need permission to take off, land, refuel, almost to sneeze, and I would have to pay a qualified mechanic to look after the works if I wanted to get a certificate of airworthiness after every ten hours' flying time. If I did not get the certificate, I could not fly.

After all that it hardly seemed to matter that in those days most of the racecourses would not allow a plane to land within an hour of the first race or take off less than an hour after the last. I reckoned that to fly to most meetings would take me so long in ground work at both ends that I would get there just as quickly by car, but when I was creeping

along in low gear and low spirits in a mile-long snake of
cars, how I wished for that Auster.

All through the winter months, and six days a week,
except of course during the snow and frost, we were on the
road, driving round the country from meeting to meeting.
In a typical week we might go to Nottingham on Monday,
return on Tuesday, go to Plumpton in Sussex and back on
Wednesday, Wincanton in Somerset on Thursday, Doncaster on Friday, home again on Saturday, and on Monday
morning the same sort of thing started again. We averaged
roughly seven hundred miles a week, though sometimes less
and sometimes much more.

I liked it. I like driving, and finding new and quieter
roads to avoid traffic and towns. All the people whose
business is racing travel these circuits too, so that one may
say goodbye to one's friends in Kent one evening, and good
morning to them the next day in Shropshire.

At each country meeting we got to know many of the
people who lived there, and could look forward to seeing
them again on our three or four yearly visits to their local
course. It is very satisfactory when one's job not only allows
but actually forces one to travel from friend to friend.

This nomadic life is one of great freedom. As long as a
jockey arrives in good time to ride in a race, or to do some
schooling, in the early morning, no one minds where he
goes or what he does. There is no office to attend, no time-
clock to be punched, no regular train to catch. Jockeys who
have become trainers look back wistfully on the days when
their work was finished with the last race and they did not
have to hurry home to worry about the horses in their care.
In the winter, when racing is very early because of the light,
the day's work is often done by half-past three and one can
relax until the next morning.

The real reason for my being a jockey, however, was not
to be found in the freedom, the friendships or the travelling
that I enjoyed, or even in the great satisfaction of winning
races : and it was not in the means it gave me of earning a
living either, for if I had been a millionaire I would still

have been a jockey. The simple fact is that I liked riding horses, and I liked the speed and challenge of racing.

I cannot explain why all jockeys, amateurs as well as professionals, are happy to take pain, cold and disappointment in their stride as long as there are horses for them to race on. Why do people climb mountains, or swim the Channel? Why do people swing on trapezes, or explore potholes? Because they can, they want to and, in some obscure way, they feel they must.

SIX

Riders and Routine

Steeplechase jockeys are a companionable crowd of men, down to earth and comfortable to be with. Most of them have a strong sense of humour and a realistic view of life.

Contrary to widespread public belief they live a quiet and sober life, for they must keep very fit if they are riding day after day. At the beginning of the season, when no one is properly fit, the jockeys come back from their August races panting more than the horses. Even after months of riding, a very hard finish or a difficult horse will try one's stamina dearly, so that one's legs feel weak and wobbly on the ground again and one's fingers tremble with fatigue as they undo the girth buckles.

Late nights and large amounts of rich food would soon soften them into useless passengers, and too much alcohol would slow their reactions and judgement, and hinder the healing of bones and cuts. So they sleep early and eat little and save their excesses for special days and the summer months.

Strangers were often surprised when they found out I was a jockey.

'You are too tall,' they said, or 'You don't look like a jockey.'

Very few steeplechase jockeys do look like jockeys. Unlike most flat-race jockeys it was no physical accident of size which chose their occupation for them, except perhaps in the case of those who started on the flat but grew too large for the job. These men are certainly shorter than average, but not nearly as small as flat jockeys; and some of them are unlucky because although they grew too big for the flat, they hardly grew tall enough for steeplechasing.

Too heavy for flat-race weights, they often have to carry a lot of lead in hurdle races and 'chases, and their short legs are a disadvantage to them over big fences – the longer the legs, the more there is to balance with.

This principle affects the whole style of steeplechase riding. The short stirrup, knees-under-chin crouch of the flat jockey, while it may be effective over hurdles, is heading straight for a fall if clung to over fences; long legs can grip better and kick a horse into a fence more strongly, and there is more feeling of being one with the horse.

Most steeplechase jockeys are between five feet six and five feet ten inches tall, with one or two six-footers, and are in every way normal men. There is nothing about their faces, their clothes, or even their non-bandy legs to proclaim their profession. Just after he won the Grand National in 1955 on Quare Times, Pat Taaffe appeared in the television programme 'What's My Line?' The newspapers were on strike at the time, so the panel of guessers had not seen any pictures of him or of the race. In spite of their practice and perception in guessing people's occupations they did not guess Pat's, and when they were told who he was, they said almost in chorus, 'But he's so big.'

Steeplechase jockeys have to be reasonably big and strong because their job is controlling large and very powerful horses. Some horses have light mouths and respond easily to a movement of hands on the reins, but others nearly pull your arms out, so every jockey who rides a great deal develops heavily muscled shoulders and back. It is almost possible, from looking at a jockey's torso, to tell how long he has been riding, like calculating the age of a tree from the rings of growth in its trunk.

Apart from their common fitness and devotion to their job, steeplechase jockeys vary as individuals as much as any random group of men would do. They touch all points from recklessly wild to intensely sober, from sensitive intuition to coarsest speaking, and from mercurial spirits to chronic envy. Some of them have a tough and ruthless sense of justice which can be disconcerting to people who are used to the British habit of suffering insult and indignity in silence.

It is often very amusing too.

One evening many years ago Tim Molony and Dave Dick parked their cars and went into an hotel in a seaside town, but the inviting stretch of kerb where they left their cars was normally reserved for taxis, which were all away at the time. Later in the evening, when Tim and Dave left the hotel, they found that the taxis were back, and all the tyres of their own cars were flat. The taxi drivers, having punished the two cars which had dared to borrow their private space, had then made the mistake of underestimating the character of the cars' owners, and had retired to their shelter for a cup of tea.

Tim and Dave without more ado unscrewed all the valves of the taxis' tyres so that they all sank down gracefully on to their rims. As Tim and Dave were attending to the last one, the taxi drivers came back and surveyed the scene with amazement and wrath.

Lurid oaths rang crisply in the warm summer night, but the general drift of their remarks seemed to be, 'You can't do that to us.'

The taxi men advanced in a body towards Dave, but he and Tim picked up the nearest man and said they would sling him over the wall into the sea if there was any more fuss. The victim yelled loudly for a truce, not anxious for a midnight bathe fully dressed, and an uneasy peace was restored. Dave and Tim declared that the moral victory was theirs, however, because the taxi drivers pumped their tyres up again for them without a murmur.

As with the sons of doctors, actors, fishermen, and others whose fathers' jobs come closely into the family life, a boy is usually led to try his fortune with horses because they have been about him from childhood. Most steeplechase jockeys are either the sons of jockeys or trainers, or were born and brought up on farms, and nearly all of them were country boys. Some of the jockeys who were first apprenticed to flat-racing stables only because of their small size come from towns, but they are exceptions. All the rest have been used to hearing endless discussions about horses from their earliest days, and have come to racing through the hunting field and point-to-points, or by growing up in a racing stable and learning the job from the cradle.

To be able to ride when one is a very young child is not essential for success as a National Hunt jockey, but it is almost impossible for any boy to learn well enough if he has not started by the time he is twelve. After that age balance has to be learned instead of developing naturally, and the coordination of every muscle has to be studied instead of being instinctive.

Boys sometimes write to me to ask how they should set about becoming steeplechase jockeys, and often their letters say something like this : 'I am very keen on riding and I always go out twice a week with the riding school in the holidays. I am sixteen now and will be leaving school soon. How can I learn to be a jockey?'

I write back with the best advice I can give them, telling them to write to trainers with details of their age, weight and ability; but as I write the envelopes and realize that they live in cities or suburbs where their gardens are too small for them to have ponies of their own, and the built-up surroundings are hopeless for riding in, I know they have no chance.

I wish I could send them a copy of a talk I once heard on the wireless. A celebrated impersonator was explaining how he graded voices into types and accents when he studied them, and into low, middle and high registers for pitch. It was a fascinating and technical explanation, and was inspiring me to try his methods and imitate hundreds of voices as incredibly as he does, when at the end he said, in a kind voice : 'There is just one more thing. You must start practising when you are five.'

With mimicry, as with every other occupation which needs some trained physical skill as well as mental ability, an early start must clearly be made. When he is eighteen a young man may decide to be a doctor or a lawyer, but it is too late for him to think about being a pianist or a jockey.

Before anyone decides to be a jockey, as well as assessing honestly his own ability, he ought to be quite clear about three things.

First, he must not be swayed by the glamour which jockeys seem to have for some people, for glamour is always in the eye of the beholder; when one has got used to wearing brilliant shirts and being stared at, all feeling of glamour fades away, but the mud, sweat and bumps are left.

Second, he must realize that luck plays a colossal part in determining the success or failure of a jockey, and that good luck does not come automatically to a good rider. I was extremely lucky, but another amateur who started when I did and became a professional at the same time and with the same sort of prospects broke his leg in his first professional race, was away for months while it mended, and never managed to re-establish himself afterwards, for other men were riding all his former mounts.

Third, he should not expect to earn a great deal of money, for out of roughly four hundred holding a licence, only about forty jockeys earn their living by racing fees alone.

I find there is a widespread misconception about jockeys' earnings, which are popularly supposed to be astronomical. For some flat-race jockeys this may be so, because they are given large retainers and there is more stake-money for flat races, but it is quite different for National Hunt jockeys.

I was one of the lucky ones. I rode a good number of races each season, was retained by two stables, and had as patrons sporting and generous owners who rewarded me well when I won and did not curse me too much when I lost. Therefore I am describing the financial aspect of a jockey's life in no spirit of personal complaint.

Very few National Hunt stables offer a retainer, because there are so many jockeys that there is nearly always a good one available. Jockeys sometimes refuse small retainers, saying that because of them they are not free to ride and perhaps win a big race on a better horse than the one they are obliged to partner, and that they are worse off in the end.

At the present time a regular fee of fifteen pounds is paid to every professional jockey riding in any race under National Hunt rules, whether he wins or loses. It is paid through the organization of Messrs Weatherby and Co, and not directly from owner to jockey. In this way jockeys are certain of being paid for their services, and are not reduced to having to ask the few unscrupulous owners over and over again for their money.

Out of this fee a jockey pays his heavy expenses, and also his contribution towards the accident fund for helping injured riders.

Flat-race jockeys have their travelling expenses given to them by the owners they ride for (through Weatherby's), but jumping jockeys pay their own. Theoretically National Hunt jockeys also claim for their journeys, but none do nowadays though it was once the normal thing. There are also valets' fees and kit replacements carving large chunks out of a jockey's income.

About forty jockeys ride more than a hundred races in a season. Of these, only ten or twelve ride more than two hundred. Roughly five hundred and sixty others race less than a hundred times. Very simple arithmetic will show that no one gets rich on riding fees alone.

When I was racing his fees were all that a jockey was legally entitled to, even for winning the National. In practice, of course, the legal minimum fee for a win was usually (but not always) augmented by a present from the owner of the horse.

The size of the present depended entirely on the owner. Most gave a little over ten per cent of the stake they won on the race; the stake might be as little as £140 at a small meeting, or more than £18,000 for the National. Some owners were extremely generous and a very few incredibly mean; and the jockeys told each other which were which!

The Whitbread Gold Cup steeplechase, which was held for the first time at Sandown Park in April 1957, was revolutionary in offering large money prizes to professional riders of the first three horses. Several races during the year award cigarette boxes, whips, trophies, or, at Worcester, a coffee service, to the winning jockey.

The shaky financial prospect of the majority of jumping jockeys does not, as I know from my own experience, in any way stop a young man from wanting to be one, and I hope it never will.

Without doubt it is fun and not finance which counts most, for amateur jockeys are as keen and dedicated as anyone. They ride on exactly the same terms and in the same races as professionals, and there are also about a hundred and fifty races for amateurs only.

Some years ago a man could remain an amateur for ever and yet ride enough to be one of the leading jockeys. Lord Mildmay, who did just this, was one of the most popular men racing and no professional jockey grudged him his success or the number of horses he rode.

For a while, however, the Stewards became much stricter, and if any amateur began to ride a great deal they called him in and gave him the same choice that they gave me, of becoming a professional jockey or riding only in amateur races.

Atty Corbett, son of Lord Rowallan the Chief Scout, did not wait for the ultimatum to be presented. He had ridden for years in every sort of race as an amateur, and was one of the very best of them, when he suddenly decided to become a professional and applied for a licence. On the first day of his professional career he was in the changing-room putting on his colours for a hurdle race when a great friend of his, still an amateur, came in to change too.

Atty, using the Stewards' chief argument, said in a ferocious voice, 'What do you so-and-so amateurs think you're doing, riding in all these races and taking the bread out of the mouths of us poor professionals?'

In later years the roles have changed again. Amateurs may now ride regularly and retain their 'Mr' for ever, but any owner engaging one who has ridden more than seventy open races must pay the equivalent of the professional fee into

Weatherby's. In this way amateurs compete equally for rides, which is fairer to all.

I remember being asked, during one of my infrequent appearances at school, to write a story called 'A Day in the Life of a Rabbit'. I expect myxomatosis has changed this to a hedgehog for the modern child. A rabbit's emotions elude me as much now as they did when I was ten, but I feel fairly well qualified to embark on 'A Day in the Life of a Steeplechase Jockey', a creature who reverses the natural laws of hibernation, sleeps in the summer and comes to life in the winter.

In the days of my youth I sprang out of bed in the early dawn, declaring it was the best part of the day, and meaning it too. Now I am given to shivering my way into jodhpurs and six sweaters, with reluctant fingers and dozing eyes; but when the sun comes up over the misty hills I am still glad I am there to see it.

Muffled to the eyelashes I drive up on to the Berkshire Downs in a Land Rover and wait for the long string of horses to wind its way up from the valley. The downs are magnificent in all weathers, but in the dawn of a winter's day, with the bare dark hills rolling to the horizon and the bitter wind sweeping across with its high thin voice, they are like the beginning of the world.

The Ridgeway, the ancient road of prehistoric man, follows along the highest part of the downs, and it is still easy to stand where no traces of civilization can be seen and to wonder at the incredible fortitude of the Iron Age men who lived and travelled on these hills because the valleys were choked with forests and prowled by wild beasts, and who had no windcheaters to shield their bodies and no bacon and eggs and hot coffee waiting for them in a warm room two miles away.

The horses reach the top of the hill and stand for a while with plumes of steam flying from their nostrils while the programme for the morning's training is explained. Then off goes one party to canter or gallop, each horse according to the stage of fitness he has reached, and the rest walk round in a circle to keep warm and take their turn to jump over the schooling fences.

Teaching horses to jump is one of the most important parts of a jockey's job, and one which must never be skimped or hurried. Thorough schooling at home makes a young horse used to finding obstacles in his way so that he is not flustered when he meets them in the nervous tension of a race. It is the same principle as endless drill for soldiers : in the heat of battle they will react instinctively in the way they have been taught when they may be under such a strain that they cannot think calmly and logically.

Older horses can sometimes be helped to overcome their mistakes, but a horse often clings to his old habits and if he was allowed to swerve over hurdles when he started to race, he will often be found still crashing through the wings in novice 'chases when he is twelve years old.

When I have the opportunity of schooling a horse from the very beginning, I like to take him gently and slowly over logs and small hurdles, on and on until he has learned the length of his own stride and the distance he needs to be from a fence when he makes his spring. Some horses put themselves right naturally, some take weeks to learn it, and some never do. These last might just as well be sent home at once, for it would take a Derby winner to make up the lengths that are lost at every fence by a horse that does not know when to take off. He jumps too soon and drags his hind legs through the fence, or too late, getting too close underneath and having to go up into the air and down again; in either case the other horses do not wait for him.

As soon as a horse is jumping fluently and with confidence over small hurdles, he goes on to large hurdles or small fences. The theory and style of jumping are the same, and one can let the horse discover that the only thing he should alter is the power of his spring.

I hate to gallop a horse over schooling fences at racing pace. It seems to me that a horse at a fast canter has time

to think what he is doing, and if he knows his job it is easy
to speed him up when he is actually racing. Horses which
have fallen or been away from racing for a while are also
usually given a refresher course over schooling fences before
they race again, and even with these old hands one can go
steadily, to give them time to regain their confidence.

Schooling lasts up to an hour, according to whether there
are two or half a dozen horses to jump, and then I rattle
and slide back down the rutted tracks and unmade roads of
the downs.

Change, shave, breakfast in a hurry, kiss the children
goodbye between mouthfuls of toast and honey, and off
with Mary to the distant races, timing things so that we
arrive there not less than an hour before the first race, for
there is a good deal to be arranged before racing begins.

The weighing-room is the heart of a racecourse, for everything begins and ends there. It is a large bare room, furnished only by the scales which give it its name, and all the
serious business of the day is conducted there, bar the little
formality of the races themselves. Plans are made, plots are
hatched, reputations are dissected, and the latest batch of
blue stories from the Stock Exchange does the rounds.
Moreover, the weighing-room is warm.

Leading off the weighing-room itself are the changing-
rooms for jockeys and the Clerk of the Course's office, and an
alcove where trainers declare every horse which is going to
run, at least three-quarters of an hour before the time of the
race he is entered for.

Arriving at the weighing-room I used to make my way
through a cloud of 'Good mornings' to the changing-room, to
consult the oracle in the shape of my valet.

Racecourse valets are somewhat like theatrical dressers —
friends, confidants, and professional smoothers-of-the-way,
they push a jockey out on to the stage, as it were, on cue, and
equipped with the right properties for the scene to be played.
They care for all kit. They wash breeches, clean saddles and
boots, and take everything needed from course to course, so
that a jockey goes to every meeting knowing that his own

clothes and saddles will be there ready for him to use. When he needs new breeches they order them for him; when any-thing needs mending, they get it done. They take with them a large collection of sweaters, helmets, breeches, saddles, whips, and boots, which they lend to anyone who needs them. I was very glad to borrow these 'spares' regularly when I started and had nothing of my own, and they were always very useful if my plans were changed at the last minute and I had to go to ride in Sussex when my kit had gone to the Midlands.

The valets are the most closed of all closed shops, for although there are about twenty of them altogether, they come from only five or six families and a stranger has no chance of joining in. Fathers, sons, uncles and cousins bundle the day's dirty load into their departing cars and reappear with everything clean in the morning, and their wives at home answer the telephone and take down messages from jockeys between trips to the washing line.

Usually each valet looks after about ten jockeys in an afternoon, but at Easter and Whitsun, when there are about fifteen race meetings on the same day, there are only one or two valets at each meeting to look after forty or fifty jockeys, and the chaos is indescribable. Every ordinary day in the changing-room they make sure jockeys have everything they need and that the right colours are there for them to put on, help them if they are in a hurry, pass on all the latest news and gossip, dress them like babies when they come back in pieces from a fall, comfort them in their troubles, and come to their rescue when they are broke. How could jockeys pos-sibly manage without them?

From his valet every day a jockey discovers exactly what horses he is going to ride, for the valet is likely to be more accurate than the morning papers and has heard the very latest plans from the trainers. All racing colours are kept and cared for by the trainers, and they bring the appropriate shirts and caps with them into the weighing-room and give them to the valet of the jockey who is to wear them. If a trainer has changed his intentions and his runners and has been unable to let his jockey know, it is usually the valet who tells him about it.

When he knows what he is riding, the jockey checks through the list of horses with his valet to see if any of them need breast-plates, blinkers or pads under the saddle, how often he will need a weight cloth, and whether any of them have so small a weight to carry that in order to get down to it he will have to use a light four-pound saddle.

About now in his day a rabbit would pause for a few nibbles of lettuce or carrot, but on a racecourse, lunch and jockeys never meet. This abstinence has nothing directly to do with weight problems, but is a simple matter of physical fitness. No one can put forth his greatest effort with a full stomach, and if a rider should fall heavily after eating he would feel ill and be sick, and shiver and sweat for hours from the shock to his system.

Having no lunch does, of course, help to keep one's weight down, but most steeplechase jockeys have no trouble at all in staying light enough. The very smallest weight ever allowed in National Hunt racing is nine stone seven pounds and the upper limit is as much as thirteen stone, but in the ordinary way horses are set to carry between ten stone and twelve stone seven pounds. This weight includes the jockey himself, his clothes, the saddle with its girths, pads, and stirrups, and blinkers if the horse needs them. It does not include the bridle or the jockey's crash helmet. All the kit and trappings weigh about twelve pounds, but by using very light things this can be reduced to about six pounds.

Without any of the dieting or sessions in sweat-boxes which make miserable the lives of most flat-jockeys, I weighed a pound or two less than ten stones, and as nearly all the horses I rode seemed to have to carry seven pounds more than that, all was well.

Some of my colleagues were not so lucky, however, and one or two of them were almost permanent residents of the Turkish baths. The grim struggles of these poor souls to squeeze off an extra pound have their funny moments : Dick Black and Dave Dick once met unexpectedly in the steam-room, celebrated with a bottle of wine, and to their horror found they were both heavier when they left the Turkish baths than when they went in.

Before the race each jockey weighs himself and everything he proposes to take with him on the 'trial' scales, and if he is not as heavy as the weight set for the horse to carry, he picks up enough of the thin flat pieces of lead lying on a bench beside the scales to bring him up to the necessary weight. The pieces of lead fit into slots in a leather-and-webbing weight cloth which lies over the horse's back under the saddle.

When the trial scales tell a jockey that he weighs about half a pound more than his objective, he takes all his paraphernalia along to the main scales, to be officially weighed out for the race.

Beside the scales sit the Clerk of the Scales and the Judge who is later to decide the winner of the race. The Judge is there to make sure that he knows the colours of every jockey riding in the race, so that in a close finish he will know quickly which horse is which. He may easily be unable to see the number-cloths of two or three horses abreast, and in National Hunt racing until 1957 there were no photographs to help him. Photographs were not used on courses where cameras were installed for flat racing, and although some curious decisions were given by judges from time to time, it was generally felt that if after three miles of strenuous effort two horses could not be separated by the human eye, they both deserved to win and a dead heat was declared to be the result. Now, however, each racecourse executive may instal and use a camera if they wish, and very few do not.

The Judge, then, studies the colours the jockeys are wearing, and the Clerk of the Scales looks at his list to find out what weight they ought to be carrying and then at the scales, to see if they coincide. The scales themselves are usually in the form of a chair for the jockey to sit on, beside a large clock-face marked in pounds; this has a lone pointer swinging round it to indicate the weight on the chair, and one feels one is being weighed like a pound of sugar in the kitchen. Scales where separate weights were added slowly until their sum balanced the jockey used to be the rule, but these died out because it took such a long time to operate them.

Weighed out, the jockeys hand over their saddles to the trainers of the horses they are to ride; the trainers carry them away to put on their animals, in the saddling boxes close to the parade ring. Ten minutes before the time of the race the jockeys leave the weighing-room and go to join the owners and trainers for a few last minutes' conversation about tactics, the weather, the horse, and his prospects for the fray.

These short before-the-race meetings were the only times I ever saw some of the people I rode for, and even with those I knew well I never had an opportunity of telling them how aware I am of their supreme importance to racing.

The whole enormous industries of flat racing and steeple-chasing depend on the pleasure that owners get from seeing their horses run. Breeders, trainers, jockeys, secretaries, stable-lads, blacksmiths, bookmakers, tic-tac men, horse-box drivers, journalists, judges, starters, handicappers, clerks of scales, clerks of courses, valets, tote operators, and the men who pick up litter on the end of pointed sticks would all be on the dole if that pleasure faded away.

Pleasure it is, not profit; for it is generally agreed that the quickest way to lose a lot of money is to buy a string of racehorses. This is particularly true of steeplechasers, for they can rarely be sold to studs when their racing careers are over. Most of them are geldings or mares, and success-ful stallions are unusual. As a result, people who own steeple-chase horses do so from love of the sport; they do not expect to win large amounts and they are very pleased if their horses earn enough in prize money to pay the training ex-penses. Not very many of them do earn enough, and this is partly because the prize money for most National Hunt races is too small. Some of the larger meetings have lately offered more races worth more than a thousand pounds to the winner, and there are several races worth more than five thousand pounds to the winner, but the average is three hundred pounds, and there cannot be more than a hundred well-endowed races every season out of a total of well over two thousand.

Competing for the two thousand races in the 1955–6 season were no fewer than five thousand different horses, and as many of them won more than one race roughly two out of every three contestants did not grace the winner's enclosure. Though the statistics for every season are much the same, the horses themselves are not, and a failure one year may redeem himself the next.

Unfortunately there seems to be no sure recipe for attaining the winning minority, for even expensive well-bred, and cherished favourites have come to grief, while the most unlikely-looking bargains of the sale ring have proved themselves world-beaters.

Encouraged by the winning habits of Rompworthy, who cost Mr Dennis a hundred pounds as a young horse, and by Russian Hero, who was bred and reared by Fearnie Williamson on his farm, a man with big ideas bought an untried horse for fifty pounds and waited for his fortune to be made. He said he did not care about steeplechasing itself, and as long as he knew when the horse was going to run in his colours so that he could bet on it he did not intend to bother and go to see its races.

Contrary to all expectations, for the horse was a poor one, his fairy tale immediately came true.

He only owned the horse for a fortnight. In that time it won a race at twenty to one, heavily backed by its ignorant owner and left alone by sensible people, and ten days later it won a selling race, and was sold afterwards for a large sum. It never won another race.

His owner thought he had found a wonderfully simple way of making a lot of money quickly and soon bought two more feeble-looking animals for small sums. But the bills for training fees rolled in and the bets were lost, for the horses this time did exactly what their trainer expected of them, which was nothing. Disgusted and poorer than when he started, their owner gave them away, for no one would buy them, and took up football pools instead. (Here his chances of winning the biggest prize are slightly less than those of his being murdered : about one in four million.)

And the moral of this Cautionary Tale for Get-rich-quick Racehorse Owners? If at first you succeed beyond your wildest dreams, don't try again.

Luckily for us all, however, this sort of owner is rare, and all the others remain faithful to their fascinating but expensive sport. It costs at least as much to keep a horse in training as it does to send a child to boarding school; but of course one cannot hope to recover the school fees by judicious betting on the end-of-term examination results, or to put the child up for auction if he is a dunce.

The short parade ring conversation ends, the trainers give their jockeys a leg up, and off they go to the start. The starting stalls familiar in flat racing are not used for National Hunt racing. Instead, a strand across the course is pulled down to a catch at shoulder level, and when this is released by the starter's lever the tape flies up at an oblique angle so that the horses start off underneath it. At some small meetings the arrangements are less formal : the starter pulls a white elastic rope across the course and to start the race lets it go, so that it springs back and clears the way for the horses.

As the jockeys circle round at the starting-point, making sure their girths are tight enough and their stirrup leathers the right length, the starter calls a roll to make sure that everyone has arrived. There are no places to be drawn for in National Hunt racing and one can start from whatever position one likes. Jockeys who are eager to start on the inside can sometimes be seen holding a private race down to the start and the first there manœuvres his steed next to the rails and almost hooks his foot over them like a grappling iron, to resist any attempts to squeeze him away.

On most courses it is an advantage to start on the inside, but on some it is not the shortest way round. Several steeple-chase courses are figure-of-eight shaped and on these it is definitely quicker in the end to start on the outside, for this position at the beginning is the inside one on the long curves farther on.

At Aintree I think the best place to start is in the centre, because down the half-mile stretch going away from the stands the ground slopes gently from right to left in such a fashion that the drops over the fences are greatest near the rails, and a horse may easily lose more time making the extra effort in jumping there than he gains by being on the inside.

Horses which have never raced before should not start on the inside, either. They already have quite enough to cope with in the startling and unnerving experience of the noise, bustle and smells of their first visit to a racecourse without having to fight for a position every inch of the way. A horse might lose his confidence for ever if he were pushed into the wings by a stronger horse, or fell because he could not force himself over the fence in the small space he would be allowed, so I liked to take very inexperienced horses round in the centre or towards the outside of the field, where there is more chance of making sure that they can see the fence clearly and will not be jostled when they take off. It is time enough to go the shortest way round when the horse is used to his surroundings and capable of holding his own in the position from which everyone else is probably trying to oust him.

When the race is over the riders return to the weighing-room in varying degrees of elation and misery. The men on the first four horses have to be weighed again to make sure they are still carrying the weight they set out with, before the result of the race is confirmed. One is allowed a margin of grace on weighing in; two pounds less than the declared weight and four pounds more will be accepted, but a bigger difference on the light side will lead to disqualification and on the heavy side to a severe fine.

One jockey weighed out one day at the very lightest weight he could manage and then, because he thought the horse he was riding was so bad that there was no fear of his coming in the first four, he added a felt pad to put under his light saddle, to avoid chafing the horse's back. The race was a fiasco, the good horses fell, and to his confusion the jockey won. As he rode back he was contemplating disaster and disgrace; the pad in its original state would not have brought him over the four pounds extra limit, but the felt always soaks up the horse's sweat, becomes wringing wet, and weighs much more than when it is dry.

The jockey received the surprised congratulations of owner and trainer abstractedly, but as he brushed through the weighing-room door solved his problem by unobtrusively dropping the felt pad on the ground. His sigh of relief was barely out before a helpful bungler picked up the pad and followed him into the weighing-room waving it in the air and shouting for all to hear, 'Hey – you dropped this.'

Accepting his burden again with a weak smile and an inward curse, the jockey sat apprehensively on the scales. He weighed three and a half pounds more than when he last sat there, and although the Clerk of the Scales frowned at him he was within the legal limit.

When he stood on the trial scales privately, clad only in his breeches, he found that he himself weighed three pounds less than he had half an hour before. It is quite usual to lose a pound or two during a hard race, but he said he had sweated it all off from fear, after he had won.

The last race ridden and all effort done, everyone chews over the day's doings with sandwiches and fruitcake in the changing-room, and drinks tea to fortify himself for the journey home. When the last farewells have been shouted and the last exhaust has racketed away in the distance, peace returns to the darkening racecourse.

And Brer Rabbit goes back to his burrow.

The author, aged thirteen, on the late Bertram Mills' pony, *Edgware Silver Star*

Dick Francis receiving the Champion Hunter rosette when riding *Sir Roger* at the Richmond Royal Horse Show, 1938

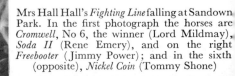

Mrs Hall Hall's *Fighting Line* falling at Sandown Park. In the first photograph the horses are *Cromwell*, No 6, the winner (Lord Mildmay), *Soda II* (Rene Emery), and on the right *Freebooter* (Jimmy Power); and in the sixth (opposite), *Nickel Coin* (Tommy Shone)

Amyclas jumping the last fence before going on to win at Birmingham, 1949

Possible jumping the last fence before winning the Molyneux Chase at Aintree, 1950

Roimond taking Becher's during the 1950 Grand National at Aintree

Silver Fame jumping the last fence before going on to win the Golden Miller Steeplechase at Cheltenham, 1950

Lochroe winning at Hurst Park, 1954

The Blindley Heath Handicap: *Devon Loch* taking the water-jump before going on to win, 1955. *Below*: Queen Elizabeth the Queen Mother watches Dick Francis ride *Devon Loch* out of the parade ring before going on to run in the 1956 Grand National

M'as-Tu-Vu at Lingfield in January 1956

Dick Francis in his paddock at Blewbury, 1972

SEVEN

Horses

I have been very fortunate, for it was my privilege to ride some great horses, including Silver Fame, Roimond, Finnure, Mont Tremblant, Halloween, Crudwell, and Devon Loch.

I hesitate to include Halloween, because I rode him only once. We parted company in mid-air, and that was that.

There can be little doubt that Silver Fame was the greatest horse Lord Bicester ever owned. He was a big, pale chestnut with a white blaze down his face, and legs with short cannon bones, built for strength. Workmanlike and wise, he thoroughly understood what was wanted of him and he never gave up fighting before he was past the winning post. If it can be believed of a horse, he had a never faltering will to win. He won the Gold Cup at Cheltenham one year in the very last stride, with Martin Molony riding him like an inspired demon up the hill, solely because of this battling quality.

Cheltenham and Sandown were his favourite courses, and Aintree was unlucky for him.

I rode him at Liverpool only once, and it was his last appearance there. He had never got farther than Becher's in the three other races he had run there, but he was entered for the Champion Chase and it was decided that he should have one more try. He gave me a wonderful ride round, jumped faultlessly and led into the last fence, a length in front of Freebooter. I can only think he was careless, for he took off at the right moment, but he brushed through the top of the fence and crashed to the ground on landing. He had fallen fast and lay still for a long time, winded. Lord Bicester hurried down the course towards us. Some fool stopped him on the way and told him his horse was dead, so he was very distressed when he reached us. Silver Fame, however, was only getting his breath back, and after a while he got up and walked off none the worse.

It is a wretched disappointment to feel oneself falling at the last fence when the race is won. Tim Molony, who rode Freebooter, believes that he would have beaten Silver Fame in any case, but I am sure he is wrong : it was almost impossible to pass Silver Fame in a long, close-fought finish, for he always found an extra ounce of strength and kept his head in front.

Two seasons later, after Freebooter had won the Grand National, the two horses opposed each other again, in the Stanley Chase at Sandown Park. There were not many other runners and the race developed into a duel between them. Jimmy Power, who had won the National on him, was riding Freebooter, and he and I went round together for most of the way. Silver Fame took a length lead three fences from home and kept it all the way up the hill to the winning post.

To have his head in front was enough for Silver Fame; he saw no point in exerting himself to win by a large margin. This habit could be disconcerting to his jockey, and it was extremely misleading to the students of form on the stands who, if Silver Fame had beaten moderate horses by a length only, got the impression that he was unfit. From poor horses, or from Freebooter, it was the same; he would win, if he could, by one length. No more, no less.

It was really unnecessary for George Beeby to give Martin or me instructions for the race when we were on Silver Fame. The horse knew it all better himself. He never forgot a course after he had run there once, and he remembered exactly at what point he had first been asked for a winning effort. Without any sign from his jockey he would quicken his stride at the right moment and take himself to the front.

I rode him one day at Cheltenham in the Golden Miller Chase. It was a four-mile race then, which meant almost three circuits of the course, and it started in the same place as the two-and-a-half-mile races. I felt Silver Fame try to start his winning run at exactly the right place for a two-and-a-half-mile 'chase. He was clearly at a loss when I pulled him back, but as we went out into the country for the third time he seemed to understand what was happening, pricked his ears, and took heart again. At the same point as before, without waiting for a sign from me, he began to race in earnest. He may have been surprised by having to go four miles, which he was not used to, for he could not manage to lead by his usual distance of one length. He only won by a head.

Lord Bicester retired him honourably from racing as soon as age began to affect his brilliance. Some horses are raced for a long time after they are past their best, and it is pathetic to see a horse that has been a world-beater running in lower- and lower-class handicaps. Silver Fame was spared this indignity. Lord Bicester took him home and sent him out hunting, but I am told he never took to it as eagerly as he had to racing.

Roimond was a horse of a different colour.

He was splendid to look at, big, strong, and well muscled, with a rich dark-chestnut coat, and he was slightly Roman-nosed. In temperament also he was completely different from Silver Fame. He was moody. Sometimes he tackled the job with a will to win, and on those occasions he was magnificent, but on other days he would set off in a race as if he were utterly bored by it all, and nothing his jockey could do would make him go any faster. Infuriatingly, he would suddenly decide to race when he got to the last half-mile, but by then it was usually too late.

Normally he was a front runner, and he wore down the opposition as one by one they made their effort to pass him, so if he lagged behind at the start and was lying sixth or eighth in the field, one knew at once that he was in one of his surly moods and he would be very unlikely to win.

He was a very good jumper, and he was so strong that even if he met a fence wrong he could crash his way through it. When he fell it was because he had underestimated the stiffness of the obstacle.

Although I always enjoyed riding him when he was in a good mood, Roimond was a very tiring horse. His back was so broad that it was like sitting astride a range of hills, and my muscles always ached afterwards.

In both of the two greatest races he ran for me he was second. One was the Grand National of 1949 when he finished behind Russian Hero, and the other was the King George VI Chase on Boxing Day at Kempton Park three months earlier.

Some of the best horses, including Cottage Rake, Happy Home, Red April, and Cloncarrig, were running in the Kempton race, but Roimond, feeling good, set off in front and led them a terrific gallop all the way. All of them tried to catch him, and in the end the greatest of them managed it. Cottage Rake joined us at the last fence, and although Roimond raced on doggedly at his former speed the Irish horse went past us to win by five lengths.

In 1951 Roimond won the Mildmay Memorial Chase at Sandown, with Tim Molony riding him. In the same race I was on another of Lord Bicester's horses, and although I could have ridden either of them I had unhesitatingly chosen Bluff King.

Bluff King, a seventeen-hands horse with enormous feet, had been especially trained for the Cheltenham Gold Cup which should have been held ten days before. The Cheltenham meeting was abandoned because of frost and snow, and the Gold Cup postponed, so it was decided that Bluff King should run at Sandown instead.

When the race started, Roimond and Tim set off in front and led all the way until the last half-mile. There Roimond seemed to be tiring, and Bluff King was still going very strongly, so I took him to the front. He led over the last fence, but he was a young horse and almost a novice still, and he would not put his head down and race; it alarmed him to be alone in front and he was trying to look round for the other horses. Also he had reached the peak of his training programme ten days before, and the interval was just enough to take the edge off his stamina. In any case, Roimond came strongly up the hill, passed Bluff King again, and won by two lengths. Tim himself was surprised at the result, and I had proved once again that a jockey often chooses the wrong horse.

Roimond ran four times in the Grand National and I rode him twice. Apart from the year when he was second, he never completed the first circuit. He fell with Dick Black and Tim Molony, and he fell with me.

The year after our near-miss, Roimond and I set off to see if we could go one better, but it was not one of his good days and he fell at the seventh fence. He had only jumped one of the first six fences well and had forced his way through the tops of the others : one cannot take such liberties with the Aintree fences without coming to a horizontal end. Over Becher's he made a colossal leap, and as he was in mid-air a press photographer clicked his camera.

It is a dramatic, a thrilling picture.

You have probably seen it : 'Players' used it for some years on a cigarette advertisement and called it 'Well ahead'. But Roimond fell at the next fence. He was not 'well ahead' for very long.

When Roimond could no longer win big races Lord Bicester sent him hunting, like Silver Fame. He took to it more successfully than the other horse, and Lord Bicester's grandson rode him in some hunter 'chases at the end of the season. It was like greeting an old friend to see him on the course again, and he looked as magnificent as ever.

It is impossible for jockeys not to have strong preferences, and of all Lord Bicester's great horses I enjoyed riding Finnure most. These feelings were not shared by Tim Molony, who championed Roimond, or by his brother Martin, who liked Silver Fame best of the three.

Finnure was a big chestnut of high quality, beautifully proportioned, and very intelligent. It gave me great pleasure just to sit on his back and look forward between his alertly pricked ears. In addition, he jumped with tremendous power, and his speed from the last fence was deeply exciting. Urging him home along the straight was like pressing the accelerator of a high-powered car; he passed everything in sight.

Before the Grand National of 1951 I rode Finnure in seven races, and he won all of them except two. On our first attempt he fell, being fresh from Ireland and unused to English fences; and he was once unplaced at Hurst Park, finding the track too sharp for him.

The five successful races included the Champion Chase at Liverpool, which he won by a length from Coloured School Boy, ridden by that excellent Aintree jockey Arthur Thompson. Arthur and I had jumped every fence side by side for two miles and it was only Finnure's burst of speed on the flat which won him the race.

His greatest trial and, I think, his greatest race ever, was the King George VI Chase at Kempton on Boxing Day, 1949. Here his chief opponent was the great Irish horse, Cottage Rake, winner of three Gold Cups at Cheltenham and, until then, unbeaten over fences in England. It was Cottage Rake who had beaten Roimond in the same race the year before, and many people considered him invincible.

During most of the race I kept Finnure in the middle of the field, going along comfortably with plenty in hand, and intending to move up to the leaders as we turned into the straight for the last time. Unfortunately Cottage Rake's jockey, Aubrey Brabazon, had the same idea at the same time, and I found myself tracking him over the last two fences.

Once over the last, half a length behind, I asked Finnure for his greatest effort, and after a terrific struggle all the way to the post he got his head in front and won by half a length.

The tremendous thrill and satisfaction of winning such a race produced a sort of choking feeling in the throat, so that between joy and exhaustion I could hardly speak when Lord Bicester greeted us in the unsaddling enclosure.

A year later, Finnure ran in the Grand National, and I

have never gone out to ride in the race with greater hope than I did that day. My splendid mount had already won at Liverpool, and had jumped round the course with confidence. I was sure he would stay the longer distance, and I thought that if all went well, his speed at the end would be decisive.

All, however, went very far from well.

There were thirty-six runners that year, and we lined up at the start waiting for one or two stragglers to come up into place when the tapes went up unexpectedly soon, and we were off. Many horses were quite unprepared for this, and had been standing flat-footed and still, so that it was a very uneven and inauspicious departure.

Finnure went off at a good gallop towards the far distant first fence. I had been told not to hurry him over the first few fences, but not everyone had the same intention. There was a panicky struggle going on among the jockeys who had instructions to stay in front and keep out of trouble – ironic advice, as things turned out. Several riders came past me with their whips up, and the race degenerated into a ragged cavalry charge up to the first fence. By the time they got there, the leaders were going so fast that they could not steady themselves to jump, and several fell. When Finnure jumped the fence with his usual éclat he landed among a jumble of men and horses lying on the ground as if it were the aftermath of a battle. He fought to avoid them, but slipped sideways, tried to recover, and fell. I picked myself up, with a deep sense of anti-climax, and joined the group of silent and disappointed jockeys standing on the course.

Eleven horses fell or were brought down at that fence : nearly a third of the whole field.

In making his gallant attempt to avoid the struggling figures on the ground, Finnure twisted his hock badly, and did not race again for over eighteen months. After this long rest he ran three times during the next season, but never regained his old speed and brilliance, and Lord Bicester finally gave him to Bruce Hobbs to use as a hack.

Bruce, who at seventeen was the youngest rider ever to

win the Grand National, rode him out for years with Cap-
tain Boyd Rochfort's string on Newmarket Heath, so the
great old fellow still had the smell of racing in his nostrils
until the day he died.

Like Lord Bicester's three horses, Mont Tremblant was
a chestnut. He belonged to Miss Dorothy Paget, and I rode
him several times one winter while Dave Dick, his usual
jockey, was recovering from a bad accident at Cheltenham
where his leg had been torn by a loose rail.

My first acquaintance with Mont Tremblant was not a
great success. Fulke Walwyn, who trained him, asked me to
school him round Newbury racecourse after the November
meeting there. I set off in the fading afternoon light with two
other horses which were being schooled, and we went round
the course satisfactorily until we came to the last fence.
Mont Tremblant met it wrong and hit it hard. I sailed over
in the air and landed on my head.

Luckily, however, no such disasters befell us when I rode
him in races. He won at Kempton, and he gave me my third
successive win in the Stanley Chase at Sandown. He was also
second in the King George VI Chase at Kempton, beaten
by Halloween. It was the third of four consecutive years that
I had been concerned in the finish of that race too.

Mont Tremblant, of course, was an accidental mount for
me, and I did not ride him in any of his greatest races. He
won the Cheltenham Gold Cup in 1952, and with Dave Dick
back in the saddle he was second to Early Mist in the Grand
National a year later.

Mont Tremblant was a beautiful horse to ride, for he
was a very deliberate jumper, and had a long, graceful
stride.

Crudwell's immense versatility was the result of his interesting breeding. His sire was Noble Star, a good long-distance
flat-racer who won many races, including the Cesarewitch,
and his dam was Alexandrina, a very successful steeplechasing mare. Few mares which have a strenuous life over fences

produce outstanding stock, but at least three of Alexandrina's foals won races.

A light-framed, brown, high-quality horse, Crudwell looked every inch a flat-racer, and he was a delicate animal who needed a lot of understanding from his trainer. Until he was eight or nine he was very difficult to feed, because he seemed to sense when he was being prepared for a race and his nervous excitement upset him. Broken bloodvessels were another of his troubles, and he bled from his nose so often that his racing career might have come to an early enforced end if it had not been found possible to prevent it by injections before every race.

For two years, as a three- and four-year-old, Crudwell ran on the flat. He won several races, and he was not disgraced by finishing second in the Ascot Stakes and third in the Great Metropolitan at Epsom. He would probably have continued in flat races if his owner, Mrs D. M. Cooper, who had bought him as a foal, had not been impatiently waiting for him to be old enough for hurdling and steeplechasing.

He took to hurdling as if it were what he had been born for, and won consistently for two more seasons.

I rode Crudwell for the first time in 1952, when I had begun to ride regularly for Frank Cundell, who trained him. Crudwell was entered for the Henry VIII Novices Chase at Hurst Park, one of the best novice races of the year, but as he had never run over fences, Frank thought he should start in an easier contest. However, I had been so impressed by the horse when I had ridden and schooled him at home that I managed to persuade Frank to change his mind, and with Mrs Cooper's blessing we set off.

When I rode Crudwell on the downs I had had a rare tremor of excitement, an intuition that our partnership held great promise for both of us. It was the sort of recognition of each other that leads to friendship between man and man, and to an unwavering understanding between man and horse. This sort of sympathy seems to have no particular cause, and no one can really explain it. It just happens.

The Henry VIII Chase confirmed my impression. I knew

lengths before we came to a fence what Crudwell was going to do, and it seemed that he was aware of it. Although it was his first steeplechase he jumped the larger obstacles without fuss, and we went round quietly, towards the back of the field, until we turned into the long straight for the last time.

Here, when I asked him, Crudwell started to fly. One by one we passed the other horses; his long, smooth run took us to the front, and he won by two or three lengths without any great exertion.

The pattern of slow start and flying finish was unchanged for three seasons. Crudwell could produce a tremendous burst of the speed which had won him his flat and hurdle races, but he did not like to be in front until he was coming into the last fence. Often his habit of trailing lazily along at the rear of the field deceived most people into thinking that he was not as good as he was supposed to be; but of our first ten races together, we won nine.

At Birmingham in February every year there was always a four-mile 'chase often used as a trial by horses preparing for the National in March. One year an Irish horse called Churchtown came over to England especially for the race, and Crudwell was also entered. It was one of Crudwell's greatest efforts. After four miles, in heavy going, he came up to Churchtown at the last fence and, although he was carrying over a stone and a half more weight, he got his head in front half-way to the post and, in a gruelling battle, kept it there until we had safely won.

Just when Crudwell was popularly supposed to be getting past his best he won the Welsh National at Chepstow. He had run in it the year before, but had been badly baulked by a falling horse when he was making his fast finishing run, and had not been able to pick up enough speed afterwards to get to the front.

Devon Loch and the Grand National were still an ache in my mind when Crudwell and I set off ten days later for our second try at the Welsh National.

As he had grown older his finishing speed had not deserted him, but he could no longer risk lying too far back during the early stages of the race, so I planned to take him gradually to the front and not leave him too much to do at the end.

All went well until the third last fence, where Crudwell made a slight mistake. He jumped the next fence very cautiously, and two horses, both carrying very light weights, which had been level with us, went on in front. As we followed them over the last fence I thought there was little hope of catching them again, but Crudwell fought on with his old flying speed and won the race in his last few strides.

Dear Crudwell. I forgot Devon Loch for the rest of the day.

Although Crudwell ran in the Cheltenham Gold Cup, and other big races, he usually did not do very well in them, and in that respect might be held not to qualify as a great horse. But any horse that has won more than fifty races of all types, from flat races to four-mile steeplechases, has proved himself to be outstanding. In 1957 he broke the record, and eventually won more races under National Hunt rules than any other horse this century. On Crudwell, in January 1957, I won for the last time.

EIGHT

Courses

Horses for courses. One hears it said so often.

Some horses have extraordinarily strong preferences for one or two tracks, or for left-handed or right-handed courses only, or for hard or soft going, or for sun on their backs, and a wise trainer does not try to lay down an opposite law. Put a horse on a track he likes, on going he likes, with a jockey he likes, and he will be worth a stone and ten lengths by the finish.

For an island the size of Great Britain, the number of steeplechase courses we have is colossal, for there are forty-five on which National Hunt meetings are regularly held. Even so, since the beginning of the century the number of courses has been steadily decreasing.

Gatwick, Derby, Rugby, Hawthorn Hill, Pershore, Colwall Park, Monmouth and Bridgenorth were war casualties in 1939, and Newport only survived for a few seasons afterwards. More recent closures have been at Beaufort Hunt, Buckfastleigh, Hurst Park, Woore, Rothbury, Manchester, Birmingham and Bogside, but the new jumping course at Ascot has added lustre to the list.

Bangor-on-Dee, ten miles over the border, is the only course in Wales now, since Chepstow in Monmouthshire reluctantly became English. Even the Welsh Grand National is expatriated. Tenby, Cardiff, Carmarthen, and Glamorgan Hunt have all expired.

There are no meetings in Cornwall, and only two Devonshire courses, Newton Abbot, and Devon and Exeter at Haldon, are healthily surviving; mainly because they are close together and hold their meetings in the same weeks in August and September, so that it is convenient for trainers

to send their horses down to stay for a while and run in
several races without making long journeys in between.
Totnes, Plymouth, and Torquay are also dead.

There are no meetings in Dorset, Hampshire (Bourne-
mouth died in infancy), Essex (Chelmsford gone), or Suffolk
(Bungay defunct).

Kent is hanging on by its eyebrows with a few days at
the beautiful course at Folkestone, and the very small but
well attended one-day meetings at Wye. Norfolk has four
days a year at Fakenham, and Lincolnshire is only repre-
sented by Market Rasen. Scotland now has only three
courses.

The enormous variety of the construction and landscape
of the courses keeps a jockey wide awake. There are hills,
sharp corners, unrailed fences, awkward landings, cross-
over courses, tan- or cinder-covered roads, and indistinct
marking flags, all to be reckoned with.

The regulations for the constitution of National Hunt
courses allow a lot of freedom. Maximum and minimum
standards are laid down, but between their limits each racecourse executive can choose widely and make a soft, easy
course or a severe one, according to their needs or beliefs.

I think it might be useful to make clear what the basic
requirements are, and as I can certainly not put it as lucidly
as the rules themselves, I will quote them word for word.

Rule 44. In all steeplechase courses :
(*a*) All fences, except those at water-jumps, must be not
    less than four feet six inches in height.
(*b*) In the first two miles there shall be at least twelve
    fences, and in each succeeding mile at least six fences.
(*c*) For each mile there shall be at least one ditch six feet
    wide and two feet deep on the take-off side of a fence,
    guarded by a bank and rail not exceeding two feet in
    height.
(*d*) There shall be a water-jump at least twelve feet wide
    and two feet deep, guarded by a fence not exceeding
    three feet in height. (The water-jump may be re-

garded as one of the fences prescribed by section (*b*).)
Rule 45.

In all Hurdle Race Courses there shall be not less
than eight flights of hurdles in the first two miles, with
an additional flight of hurdles for every completed
quarter of a mile beyond that distance, the height of
the hurdles being not less than three feet six inches
from the bottom bar to the top bar.

I have ridden races on most of the different courses and
in my mind have always sorted them out into two main
categories, flat and hilly. (The official term for hilly is
'undulating'.) These I subdivided into flat and easy, flat and
difficult, hilly and easy, and hilly and difficult. The divisions
are my own personal opinions, and other jockeys may
thoroughly disagree with me.

Every race, as I have probably said only too often, is an
individual event, never repeated and rarely predicted. It is
not possible to find universal rules about horses, and if you
know an exception to every generalization I make, I would
not be surprised.

The rough classification of courses which follows refers
to steeplechase tracks only. Hurdle-race tracks do not vary
nearly so much, for although they have their own problems
of hills and sharp corners, the obstacles themselves are the
same everywhere.

Flat and easy		*Flat and difficult*
Bangor-on-Dee	Southwell	Aintree
Catterick	Stratford-on-Avon	Doncaster
Hereford	Taunton	Haydock Park
Cartmel	Uttoxeter	Kempton Park
Huntingdon	Wincanton	Newbury
Kelso	Wetherby	
Ludlow	Windsor	
Market Rasen	Wolverhampton	
Newton Abbot	Worcester	
Nottingham	Wye	

Hilly and easy	Hilly and difficult	Courses I have not ridden on
Folkestone	Devon and Exeter	Ascot
Fontwell Park	Cheltenham	Ayr
Lingfield	Chepstow	Carlisle
Plumpton	Hexham	Perth
Warwick	Leicester	Sedgefield
	Plumpton	Newcastle
	Towcester	Fakenham
	Sandown Park	Teesside Park

Flat and easy courses, the majority, are those which present no special difficulties. They are very fast tracks when the ground is dry, and the fences are inviting or easy to jump. If the circumstances are normal, and one's horse is good enough, it is prudent to lie within six or seven lengths of the leaders, for few horses have enough speed to make up more ground than that against good opposition. It is a different matter, perhaps, if one is astride a Pegasus among Percherons, but even then it is foolish to take risks. Hares with too much confidence have given tortoises the race before now.

In nothing shorter than a four-mile race can one safely allow one or two horses to set off at a sprint without going after them, but even on a level course they will wear themselves out after three miles at flat-out speeds and will have no strength left to hold off the steadier gallopers behind.

Some horses definitely run best when they are in front and have a clear view ahead. They may be one-speed animals whose best hope is to set a good gallop from the start and take their opponents along so fast that they have no reserves left for catching them at the end, or the useful sort of horse which dislikes being passed and puts in a fresh spurt every time he hears hoofbeats at his quarters. It is as exasperating trying to pass one of these excellent creatures as it is getting by a road-hog who suddenly drives faster when one draws alongside.

Hurst Park was a wonderful course for front runners.

The straight was about half a mile long and all the rest of
the course was a gently curving circle, so that from the air
it would look like a D. The fences were pleasantly easy, and
the ground drained quickly because the course was on the
bank of the Thames. Looking backwards from the top of
the stands one had an interesting view, over the boundary
fence, of barges and rowing eights holding unintentional
races on the river.

The English record for a three-mile 'chase was set up at
Hurst Park by the great Galloway Braes in May 1953, when
he covered the course in five minutes, forty-seven and four-
fifths seconds. He was always at his best in front, and the
races he ran at Hurst Park, when he slipped the field on the
last part of the circle and drew farther and farther away
down the straight, had the stands gasping with sheer excitement and his opponents with frustrated amazement that
anything should show them so clear a set of heels.

I knew those heels well. One day I followed Galloway
Braes for three miles round Fontwell without a hope of
catching him, and I was riding Crudwell, who was a flyer
himself. Indeed we drew so far ahead of the other two runners as I pursued the never-tiring champion that there was
a real danger of all four horses coming together with a
resounding crash in the cross-over part of the figure-of-eight
course, two of us having gone round the bottom loop while
the other two were still jumping the top one.

Hurst Park was always a lucky course for me, though
not my favourite, because I have a soft spot for bigger
fences. It was in two days there, and the following day at
Sandown, that I put up my own super-colossal four-star
record of eight wins in eleven rides.

The 'flat and difficult' courses are primarily those with big,
stiff fences and they are only difficult on a moderate horse.
A good bold jumper takes them with no trouble at all, and
on the back of one of these the flat and difficult courses are
a pleasure to ride on. One gets a much more definite feeling
of lift and flight when the fences are big : and, if one's horse

is clumsy, an equally definite, but less enjoyable feeling of falling off a cliff.

The Grand National course at Aintree is the extreme example of this type of track. It is very flat, so that one has no hill-climbing problems, and the only difficulty in the lie of the ground is the varying state of the going when there has been a good deal of rain shortly before a meeting. The racecourse proper and especially the run-in from the last fence remain soft, while out in the country the course drains into the brook and the canal and dries very quickly. It is disconcerting for some horses, especially those which have never been hunted, to gallop from firm on to sticky ground and they often flounder when they come round to the straight, using up the energy they need for a second circuit.

In very dry weather, on the other hand, the excellent and more rarely used turf out in the country is still springy, while the racecourse itself, with its well-worn grass, is inclined to be firm.

There are two separate steeplechase courses at Aintree. The second course was constructed in 1952 and was named in honour and memory of Lord Mildmay.

Just under a mile and a half round, the new course runs beside and across the hurdle track, on the stands side of the Melling Road. As the Mildmay course was designed to be an introduction to Liverpool and a preparatory school for the big fences, its obstacles look small editions of the National ones. All of them are entirely covered with green branches of spruce, fern and gorse.

On no other courses are the fences green all over, though many places face the bottoms with evergreen so that the horse's eye travels smoothly from the turf to the fence, which encourages him to jump. Some of the Midland meetings do not use evergreen and although the fences are good to jump they appear black and staring as one approaches them.

Two fences are common to both the Mildmay and National courses: the water-jump, and the second last of the National, which is the third last of the Mildmay. These two are the only taste a horse gets of the drops on the landing side awaiting him on the longer course, and the plain 'National' fence, sandwiched unexpectedly in the straight, often causes trouble.

The other Mildmay fences, though smaller, are very hard, and one cannot take liberties with them. Although this does have the desired effect of making the horses try to clear them, it is my own feeling that it would be better to raise them a few inches and make the tops comparatively soft, so that they would more closely resemble the construction of the National fences.

The National course is nearly two and a quarter miles round, and the last fence is over a quarter of a mile from the winning post.

The ground level on the take-off side of each of the sixteen fences is higher, sometimes by as much as two and a half feet, than it is on the landing side. On ordinary courses a man can stand behind a fence and see the track over the top of it. At Aintree he would need to be on stilts to do it. As one gallops between the fences on the straight to Becher's, one can see the horses in front disappear as they jump, and then just the caps of the jockeys bob into sight as they set off again to the next obstacle.

On no other course is this feature so constant and so marked, and it is the drops taken at racing pace, more than the actual size of the fences, which are the chief hazard at Liverpool.

Although British racehorses are generally unused to them, a slight but not exaggerated drop is helpful to a horse, for it gives him extra time to stretch his feet out before he touches the ground. Fences where the landing side is higher than the take-off side are so likely to bring a racing horse down that great care is taken by every course to see that they do not exist.

Given a good horse and a clear run (a combination devoutly to be wished but seldom granted), there is a perfect path round Aintree like a firm but hidden way through a quicksand.

As I said before, I think the centre is the best place to

start from in the National, because the drops are greatest near the rails. The centre has two other big advantages. It is a not unknown fact that horses fall in the National, and once they are loose they gallop unpredictably about, causing awkward situations for everyone else. If one is in the middle of the course one can go either to the right or the left to avoid visible trouble ahead, but if one is on the rails, a horse falling or veering into one leaves no chance of escape.

The centre also brings one into the best position for negotiating the bend after Becher's and the sharp left-hand turn at the Canal.

Becher's, the sixth fence down the long straight away from the start, should be jumped at a fair speed. The famous brook runs along under the landing side of the fence, and its far bank slopes sharply up to the level ground. It is easy to imagine what happens to a horse which takes off too slowly and too close to the fence : he comes down on to the sloping bank of the brook, and from there on to his nose. One's only hope at Becher's is to clear the brook completely, and the faster one is going the farther into safety one should land.

The course starts to bend to the left immediately after the fence, but if one jumps it in the middle the curve is almost unnoticeable.

The next fence, the seventh, is in a slight dip, and is the only one where the take-off side does not lead up to the fence like a ramp. If one's horse does not stand back from this fence to jump it, there is no need to worry about any fences farther on : one's progress is apt to come abruptly to a full stop. Twice in the National I have proved it.

The Canal Turn is next, and it is at this fence especially that the centre position is a great advantage.

The Turn is literally a right angle, and the fence is on the edge of it like a white-line Halt sign at a T junction with a main road. Ahead is the Canal, to the left is the course. If one jumps this fence on the inside the turn is so sharp that one either swings wide or slows down to avoid the horse tangling its feet up in a pirouette. As one approaches in the centre one can persuade one's horse to jump across at an angle instead of straight ahead, and as he lands he is already facing the way he has to go. This little crab-like manoeuvre is extremely easy on horses which are naturally inclined to jump to the left.

On the landing side, after such a diagonal jump, and down the short stretch to Valentine's, one is automatically slightly nearer the rails, but still not next to them.

Valentine's has not quite as severe a landing slope as Becher's, but it needs much the same treatment for it is the same brook, which runs across the whole course and drains into the canal.

The next three fences need no more than ordinary care. They all have drops, but here they are not greater near the rails and one can gradually work one's way over to within twelve feet or so of the inside. As one comes towards the Melling Road again the course bends very slightly to the right; if one continues in a dead straight line one finds the rails drawing nearer.

The tan-covered Melling Road is shut off by big level-crossing type gates which swing back across the course on non-racing days. Galloping over the road one comes on to the racecourse proper and into the wide-open space where four courses join and cross and where the Grand Sefton and Foxhunters steeplechases start.

Luckily there are some wooden dolls showing the way, for the mouths of four roads to the winning post are open in front of one. If any newcomer to the course ever finds himself in front and the dolls have been forgotten, he should not take a short cut down the flat-racing five furlongs, and should avoid turning sharply to the left because he will find himself going backwards over the Mildmay course or the hurdles; but he should take the left-hand fork of the trident facing him. Down there he will find two plain fences : the thirteenth and fourteenth of the first circuit, and the last two in the National. Over these fences and on past the stands one can safely cling to the rails.

The Chair, in front of the stands, is, I think, the most

difficult of the whole course, because of its height and spread and its formidable appearance. Horses often fall there in the Topham Trophy and other races when it comes near the beginning, but in the National only good jumpers usually survive the rigours of the two-mile circuit to reach it, and they are also by then used to the enormous size of the fences. Mercifully, after the extra effort to jump it, there is hardly any drop to complicate the landing.

The last fence of the last circuit is the water-jump and this, to me, is the easiest of them all. Although it is slightly wider than most water-jumps, the drop in this case is helpful, because the horse can concentrate on stretch and does not have to trouble about height.

As close now to the rails as one can get, one swings round to the left, under the starting gate and on towards the first, now the seventeenth fence. It is roughly four hundred yards away and during the gallop towards it one can take a gently oblique line back to its centre, ready to start the whole course again.

At the end of the second circuit the run-in from the last fence leads across the main 'chasing course and on to the parallel hurdle track, where the straight runs alongside the Chair and the water-jump to the winning post.

Next to the Aintree fences in size and, to me, enjoyment, are those at Kempton. Big awe-inspiring obstacles with marked landing drops, many novice 'chasers find them too overpowering, and it is not a good course for any but courageous jumpers.

The wings of the fences, though long, were lower than those on other courses, and this had the effect of making the fences look even bigger than they were. Normally, wings are considerably higher than their fence, but at Kempton they stood barely eighteen inches above the birch. However, the fences are all built with such a steep slope away from the approaching horses that it is almost impossible to get too close to them. Even if one's horse takes off with his feet rapping the bottom bar of a fence, a risky position on most courses, at Kempton the slope allows him a few precious inches of space to lift his tucked-in forelegs over the top.

The fences are exceptionally stiff. They are packed tight uncompromisingly to a few inches above the regulation minimum of four feet six, and horses that are used to brushing their feet carelessly through the tops of fences soon change their minds about it if they are still going at the second.

Jockeys at Kempton fall off for what looks from the stands to be no reason at all, and are roundly cursed for their clumsiness. But what happens is that a horse, taking off too soon, hits the top of the fence with his belly as he is coming down. He may land safely, though slowly, on the other side, but his jockey has described a delicate parabola in the air and is now nursing bruises and a grievance on the ground. The unyielding birch has done its deadly work of acting like a jammed-on brake in a car : the passengers in the back seat fall forward on to the front seat, and the driver's companion puts his head through the windscreen. The jockey goes over the head of his horse and no skill of his can reverse the laws of nature.

Some years ago I rode a well-backed horse in a novice 'chase at Kempton. It would be more correct to say that I intended to ride him, for, to the dismay and fury of his supporters, we pulled up, for no apparent reason, before we arrived at the second fence. As we went over the first fence the horse, who was a good hurdler, made a long low jump, saw he was not high enough, made a convulsive effort in mid-air, scraped his belly through the top of the fence, and landed safely. But the awkward jump and the stiff birch had between them taken his saddle back, giving me no choice but to pull him up as quickly as I could. Riding a racehorse on a slipping saddle is like trying to sit on a greasy pole.

Ever afterwards the horse wore a breast-plate – an extra strap looped round the girths and running upwards between the horse's forelegs to a ring at the base of his neck. From here another strap circles his neck, and this in its turn is held in place by two short side straps which run to the front edge of the saddle just below the pommel.

So many horses of small girth tend to jump clear through their saddles that I tried always to persuade trainers for whom I rode to let me use a breast-plate as a normal part of my kit. Some, like Mr Peter Cazalet, used them regularly long before I appeared on the scene.

A breast-girth is not the same thing as a breast-plate, and I do not think it is as good. A breast-girth is a strap which runs loosely from the girths where they join the saddle, round the base of the neck of the horse, and back to the saddle. Its weight is supported in front by a narrow strap running over the top of the horse's neck in front of his withers. Although it stops the saddle going backwards it does not hold the girths in place underneath. A horse can still jump through the girths, loosen the saddle, and make the man on top thoroughly insecure. The horse also pulls the weight of saddle and rider on his chest, and obviously cannot race at his fastest.

Many a good chance has been lost on a slipped-back saddle and, apart from the horrible feeling and the prospect of being unceremoniously dumped on the ground, it is the needlessness of the disaster which is so annoying. However tight the girths are pulled before the race, an extended galloping horse can loosen them, and with such a simple and effective device as a breast-plate to hand it is amazing to me how many trainers still take this risk of not using one.

Hurdlers do not perhaps need a breast-plate so much, and nor do horses which have summered well and are fat around the middle.

Some jockeys, trying to do a light weight, persuade the trainer against his better judgement to leave off the breast-plate, because it weighs about a pound : but I think one needs a breast-plate even more with a small postage-stamp saddle, and the extra pound may be worth its weight in fivers.

I have classed Doncaster, Haydock Park, and Newbury courses as 'difficult' mainly because of their size. All of them have exceptionally long and wide straights, and it is easy to make mistakes with one's final effort. The winning post, by a foreshortening optical illusion, always looks nearer on a wide course than it really is, and there is a great temptation to loose one's horse too soon. An inexperienced rider may arrive at the front only to find that the winning post is still on the horizon, and that other more patient jockeys are sitting with double handfuls behind him, ready for the kill.

On the other hand, it is fatal to wait too long, and no jockey looks more foolish, or suffers more abuse, than the one who finishes at great speed but fails by a length to overhaul the winner in time.

All three courses have big, stiff fences, and I have observed that they always look bigger when one is riding a poor jumper.

Down the far side of the course at Haydock there are drops to the fences very like those at Aintree. Indeed this course, nearest on the map to Liverpool, is a good preparation for the big test, and since the war Sheila's Cottage, Russian Hero, Freebooter and E.S.B. all won races at Haydock before they won the National.

Haydock is one of the few courses where it does not pay to come over the last fence close to the rails. Straight ahead are an open ditch and the water-jump, and the way to the winning post veers fairly sharply to the right to avoid them. By jumping the last fence towards the outside and going straight on one finds oneself close to the rails again a hundred yards later.

Both Haydock and Newbury are officially described as 'undulating' because of a slight dip at one stage of an otherwise flat course. On the other hand, the new course at Ascot, though officially 'flat', has a severe pull up from Swinley Bottom. The last six fences are all built on this rising ground, and I'm sure it must seem never-ending to a tired horse.

'Hilly and easy' courses are those where the inclines are not too steep or do not occur near the winning post. Most of them have short circuits. Fontwell Park and Plumpton are little more than a mile round; but Warwick, the exception, is deceptively as long as Doncaster.

Warwick racecourse runs up and round the lower slopes of a sharp little hill rising in the centre of the course, and except from the very top of the stands the horses are lost to view behind it for over a furlong. They sweep down off the hill along the back straight, and the rest of the course is flat.

In spite of the hill, in dry weather the track is a fast one, and the English record for a two-mile hurdle was put up there by Shahjem in December 1955. In wet weather the course drains very patchily, and the fence at the foot of the hill often has to be missed out because water collects and lies around it.

At one meeting at Warwick there was an alarming and unusual number of falls. Some of the fences had been entirely and stiffly rebuilt, while others had not needed such fundamental repair; but one could not tell from looking at them which was which. The horses soon found out. Brushing lazily through the tops of the old fences they suddenly came to a new one and hit it with a bang.

Except to the victims it was an interesting and informative meeting, for it proved without a doubt that whereas horses can adapt themselves to a different construction of fences on separate courses, they expect all the fences on one course to be alike.

Lingfield is one of the pleasantest of all courses to ride on. The fences are beautifully built and very wide, and the high wings make them so inviting that one almost feels like jumping them oneself without bothering to take a horse along too.

The one hill is well away from the finish, and although it is a steep pull up to the top, there is then a fast downhill stretch before one sweeps round the final curve into the straight. As with all the 'hilly and easy' courses the extra speed one can achieve going down the slope more than makes up for the effort of getting to the top of it.

'Hilly and difficult' courses like the 'flat and difficult', are long galloping tracks with big fences. On all of them the finishing line is on or just after an up-gradient, and there is no freewheeling run-in for a tiring horse.

The hills at Lingfield, Plumpton, and Devon and Exeter are the steepest in the country, but they are so far from the finish in each case that one can take a breather going up and at the top before gathering one's forces for the final effort. At Towcester, however, on the fourth most severe slope, there is no respite for horse or man, because the winning post is at the top of a heart-straining climb. The last three-quarters of a mile is unrelentingly uphill, with three fences, including an open ditch, to be conquered on the way.

On soft going many horses are so tired by the time they get to the last fence that they are almost walking over it, and some of the world's slowest finishes must have been fought out on the run-in.

Meetings at Towcester are all held in the spring and autumn so, although it is sometimes heavy, the going is never deep enough to ask cruel or impossible labours from the runners there.

I have had to put Plumpton in both 'hilly' columns because I could not decide which it should properly belong to. For many years I would unhesitatingly have called it difficult, but one day I rode Domata there, and it was a revelation. Domata jumped the course with the utmost ease, gaining lengths at every fence, and winning on the strength of it, for, as it was his first run of the season, he was not fully fit.

It occurred to me that I had always thought of Plumpton as difficult because I had never been round on a really good horse. Plumpton has its virtues, but it does not usually attract the top-class stars. Had I ridden there only on Finnure, Crudwell and Lochroe, I would probably never have thought the downhill fences at all formidable. As one lands over them the ground is dropping away, so that the second or third stride from a fence may still find a horse overbalancing on to its nose.

Even though the landing side of the water-jump is flat and the fence itself is perfectly ordinary, I think I fell at it more often than at any other fence in the whole of Britain. Three times on one day I walked back, rather damp, from this farthest obstacle. Eventually it dawned on me, as I lay inspecting it from close quarters for the umpteenth time, that the landing side was less cut up away from the rails; and by jumping the fence on the outside from then on I usually managed to cross the water safely. Recent alterations to this fence, and to the worst downhill one, have made them easier to jump.

In three-mile 'chases at many courses one jumps nineteen fences instead of the minimum eighteen. At Sandown, however, everyone has extra fun for their money, because in a three-mile race there are no less than twenty-two obstacles.

Sandown has always been my favourite course after Liverpool, but working on the reverse principle from Plumpton, I think now that this may be because I have usually been round on a good horse.

The three-mile 'chases start with the horses' backs to the highest part of the course, and there is a short downhill run to the first fence.

Round the corner, along the back straight, there are seven exacting fences close together; three, then the water, then another three. Everything depends upon timing one's distance between them, like crossing the string of traffic lights on the Great West Road. If you meet the first one right you get a smooth, clear run, but if you are wrong at the first you have trouble with them all.

After these seven there is a long curve round towards the straight, and one starts to go uphill as one approaches the Pond fence, named for the giant saucerful of stagnant water which lies between the 'chasing and hurdling courses. The slope upwards is continuous past the next two fences and all along in front of the stands.

At the top, out of sight of most people in the enclosures, the horses swing right and race down beside the Members' car park, where all that can be seen of them are the jockeys' bright caps bobbing above the Daimlers, the Bentleys, and the Morris Minors.

On the second circuit the Pond fence and the two after it up the hill sort out all the tired horses. One bad mistake at any of these three fences may lose a race, because it is a strong horse which can pick up speed again after being un-balanced in his all-out climb.

After their race the horses have so long a walk back to the paddock that it is quite common for a jockey to be called out for the next race before he has got back into the weigh-ing-room to start changing. The half-hour between races, which drags along for race-goers on a cold day, is pitifully short for the mad quick-change scramble behind the scenes experienced by those jockeys lucky enough to be in full em-ployment.

Quite different are the days when one is due to ride only in the last race. The afternoon seems never-ending, and when at last one is changed into colours the winter light may already be fading, and there is a steady drift of people going home. It is all very depressing. Give me Sandown in a rush every time.

The only major steeplechase course which is not devoted to flat racing in the summer is Cheltenham, the head-quarters of National Hunt racing.

The brown and purple hills which stand in an arc round the course are justly famous, but it is little use my describing them or showing a picture of them. Landscapes have to be seen in the moving air, with the noises and smells of the earth alive in one's senses. Pictures seem dead to me. Visual memory may be defective and imagination mistaken, but the mind can recall the essence of a place, familiar, dreary, or exotic, without the help of a photograph or a painting.

On the hills at Cheltenham the changes in the light from a brilliant sparkle to a soft mist are so infinite that they could keep an artist (unsatisfactorily) employed for years.

Cheltenham, like many hilly courses, calls for sit-and-suffer tactics. Unless the winning post is at the top of an incline it is not particularly wise to ride one's horse hard uphill, for he will use in climbing the energy he needs later on for a winning run : nevertheless one feels, in easing one's mount, that time is being lost, and it is even worse when other horses sprint past. Hence the term 'sit and suffer', horribly familiar to all regular jockeys.

There are two uphill stretches at Cheltenham, one in front of the stands, and a fairly stiff one on the farther side of the course. At the top of this slope there is a gradual swing to the left on the new course, but a sharp bend on the old course. Green riders gallop fast up the hill, passing the sit-and-suffer brigade with ease, but on the old course they find their speed carrying them wide round the bend, and they at once lose the lengths they have tired their horses to gain.

From the top bend there is a long, steep, downhill gallop to the third last fence; after the next jump a fairly sharp rising curve leads round to the last fence, before one tackles the uphill finish. It is a difficult course to ride a waiting race on, because if one is not close up round the last bend, the late fast run has to be made in a short climbing rush. It can be and has been done, but on this course, more than any other, it is easy to leave a waiting-race horse too much to do at the end.

On the other hand, it is asking a great deal of a horse to expect him to lead all the way. Setting the pace up and down the hills is too much for many natural front runners which win from in front on flat courses with ease but often fail at Cheltenham.

The most notable exception I have ever seen was Lord Bicester's Royal Approach, which came over from Ireland in 1954 to run in the Cathcart Steeplechase, the last race of the Festival meeting. Ridden by Pat Taaffe, he started off in front and went farther and farther away from the rest of the field, winning by a distance without exerting himself and making the other runners look like donkeys. Tragically, the horse broke a bone in his knee while turned out at grass a few months afterwards, for he showed, at six years old, every promise of becoming another great star in

Lord Bicester's string. After two seasons' rest he raced again, but without his former signs of greatness.

From Cheltenham, Aintree and Sandown, to Cartmel, Plumpton and Wye, every racecourse has its own personality. No two are alike. Each has its own flavour, oddities and customs, and almost its own insignia, like ribbed woollen stockings at Cheltenham, rain at Haydock Park, and straw-bale grandstands at Bangor-on-Dee.

In some ways every course is the same. At the gates everywhere one is greeted by the smell of jellied eels, a glimpse of the regular tipsters, the welcoming 'Hello, Dickie boy' of Johnny, Fatty and Tishy, the newspaper sellers, and the familiar argument between the turnstile keeper and the man who is unlawfully trying to get in free.

NINE

Chase Me a Steeple

There is no one technique of race-riding which can be clung to through thick and thin, mud and concrete, ditch and hurdle, world-beater and rogue. Every course, every horse, every fence demands a constant renewal of attention, and in the variety of the challenge lies much of its abiding fascination.

Every jockey develops a personal style which is as easy to spot through race-glasses as the colours he is wearing, and many specialize in either hurdles or 'chases; but a man who unimaginatively rides every race to the same pattern, and treats every horse with the same pressure or lack of it, will sometimes lose when he might well have won.

There is always discussion about the virtues of the contrasting 'forward' and 'backward' seats, and each in turn is hotly declared to be better. A compromise of 'in the middle' is often thought to be best of all. It seems to me that each is designed for a particular job, and each is right at the right time.

The forward seat is to be seen in its most extreme form when a tall, thin horseman sits like a squashed-up 'N' over the withers of a show-jumper. The theory behind this crouch is that a horse scarcely feels the burden of his rider if the weight is balanced over his shoulder, and in modern show-jumping it has become the custom for the rider to allow himself to be thrown into the air by the horse's leap so that at the moment of greatest height he has scarcely any contact with the horse at all. It can hardly be called a graceful proceeding, but it is effective if it is done properly. Unfortunately for the large number of people who attempt it, however, it is very difficult, and calls for great skill and constant practice.

Being thrown up into the air is easy enough to manage, as I have often and unintentionally found out, but retaining a safe balance demands extraordinary control when the head is down beside the horse's mouth, the seat is in the air over his withers, and the knees are barely touching the horse. Thousands of jumps are ruined, after this point has been reached, by the rider falling back into the saddle with an audible bump. Often a horse can even be heard to make a noise somewhere between a cough and a groan when eleven stone of solid body, light as a feather at the height of the jump, suddenly knocks all the breath out of him as he is landing. Down go his hind legs, down go the poles and bricks, up goes the score of faults.

A modified form of the forward technique is useful over hurdles, but it would be suicidal to stick to the show-jumper's crouch, which is designed for accuracy and not for speed, because it does not allow one's legs to grip properly and the slightest check or twist in the horse's stride as he hit a hurdle would dislodge the jockey. The reins have to be held very short, and little allowance can be made for a horse suddenly pecking as he lands and thrusting his head down or out to recover himself. Indeed the 'bottom up' position is only seen in racing when a rider is making an involuntary descent from the saddle.

In hurdling there is no need to lift all the weight entirely off the horse, for speed and not height is the aim. It is enough if the weight is balanced where it is least trouble to the horse and safest for the equilibrium of the rider. The exact spot of this balance varies greatly from horse to horse. It is, for instance, no use trying to lean up over the neck of an indifferent jumper, but one may sit forward with confidence on the natural sort of hurdler which barely raises the height of his body from the ground when he jumps and flows over the hurdles mainly by lifting his legs higher than for a normal galloping stride.

Continental riders adopt the forward seat much more

consistently, for their hurdles and fences are soft and rarely unbalance a horse which hits them.

For a few months at the end of 1954, French hurdles were introduced into English racing. Letters were written by the thousand to sports editors about them, jockeys' opinions, however unprintable, were faithfully collected, and in every bar from Lambourn to Newmarket press comments were digested with the beer.

Normal racing hurdles are a larger edition of farmers' sheep hurdles, interlaced with gorse to make them more visible, and hammered into the ground with a mallet. Each flight, according to the width of the course, consists of from six to ten separate hurdles standing side by side but not tied together in any way, so that if a horse hits one hard enough it may be knocked flat on the ground without disturbing its neighbours. When one hurdle is broken in a race it is immediately replaced by a new one from the stack kept ready beside every flight, so that horses never have to jump damaged hurdles second time round. The top bars of the flight must be at least three feet six inches from the ground, and the hurdles all slope at a slight angle away from the approaching horses so that they do not have to face a completely upright obstacle.

The French-type hurdles were different in almost every respect. Only in height and slope were they the same. They were built in movable ten-foot sections but were so heavy that four men were needed to lift them. They were constructed of birch twigs rammed between two parallel bars eighteen inches apart and the same distance from the ground, and wired down on to a base-board. On the approach side the gap between the bar and the base was covered in with green-painted planks, so that in a race it seemed as though one was jumping a succession of green window-boxes planted thickly with two-foot-high birch twigs. The hurdles were fixed to the ground by large staples like overgrown croquet hoops, which were dropped over the ends and hammered down.

Trainers were at first in favour of the French hurdles

because they were safer for the horses' legs. Ordinary hurdles deal out harm in various ways : rapping the bars bruises a horse and may make him shin-sore, brushing through the gorse stings and leaves prickles in his skin, and breaking the wood by bad jumping may lead to the offender or any other runner suffering a badly pierced leg. Hurdles swinging back into place when they have been hit forward by one horse may tangle the legs of the horse behind and bring him down; and a rebounding hurdle is a very nasty thing to have to deal with, as I have sometimes found to my cost.

With the French hurdles, on the other hand, there was no danger from sharp wooden stakes or flapping sections. Horses could gallop over and through them with no trouble at all, and the birch did not scratch them.

At first it seemed that there could be no drawbacks to these mild obstacles, and many people thought they would become the normal thing on all courses. But gradually one became aware that their very easiness was a snare. Many a hurdler discovered that he did not hurt himself if he hit the birch and began to treat the little fences as if they were not there at all, often galloping straight over them without making any particular attempt to jump. On the few occasions when such a horse misjudged his distance calamitously, his fall was fast, hard, and dangerous.

The second bad consequence of the easier hurdles was a little longer showing itself. Not until horses which had raced over French hurdles were put to steeplechase fences was it found that they would no longer bother to jump over the top. Dozens of novice 'chasers crashed to the ground because they had tried to apply to a good hard-built plain fence the experience they had gained over hurdles. Nor could they be blamed, for apart from the difference in height the new hurdles and the old fences looked very much alike.

In France even the big fences are very soft and offer no serious resistance to horses brushing through them, so no harm is done by having soft hurdles also. It seemed clear, as the tale of riderless horses and grass-stained jockeys grew longer and longer, that if we were not to accept in Britain the French version of soft big fences, it was senseless having soft little ones.

So the experiment was over, the starch was put back into hurdle races, and the by now more popular 'forward' seat prudently retreated an inch or two.

The forward seat is, of course, used almost exclusively in flat racing. I greatly respect the flat jockeys for their sensitive timing and skill in a finish; but they have little to do in the way of complicated riding. This I am often told, not having ridden on the flat myself, by National Hunt jockeys light enough to have a few rides in the summer. Their unanimous opinion about the amount of horsemanship needed in a flat race is – very little. And, they say, very few flat-race jockeys would stay on over hurdles, so insecurely are they perched on top.

Do not mistake me. I do not wish to imply that no flat-race jockeys are good horsemen for, of course, this is not true; many of them are. But it is clear that indifferent horsemen can have great success on the flat, and little or none over hurdles and fences.

It is not easy to explain the difference between a good horseman and good jockey, but if I attempt it, it will be in the same spirit that theatre critics discuss plays and actors : they make very definite statements of what should be done without in the least being able to do it themselves. So in describing the perfections of horsemanship and jockeyship I am not implying that I myself am capable of them.

The Perfect Horseman is quiet on a horse. The calmness which springs from confidence in his own ability extends to the horse and quietens him too. Nothing frightens a horse as much as a frightened rider, and nothing will make a horse more restless and fidgety than a rider who cannot sit still. Horses are extremely sensitive to the mental state of the man on their back; some could even be thought to be two different animals, so opposite may their form be with two riders of contrasting skill and temperament.

The Perfect Horseman's legs are strong, and by using his thigh and calf muscles he can squeeze and urge his mount to go faster; but he does not wildly clap his heels against the flanks as if he were beating a drum. His hands are strong also, but with a gentle firmness that controls and guides, not a savage grip that fights a continual battle against the horse's mouth. A fierce pull will only encourage a horse to get the bit in his teeth and bolt in order to stop the jagged pain at the soft corners of his mouth.

It is a terrifying sight to see a man being run away with, for he has absolutely no control of any sort and is altogether at the mercy of his horse. The Perfect Horseman is never run away with. But he sometimes cannot stop when he wants to !

A few horses are such strong pullers that they can over-rule any halt signs from the saddle, while remaining amenable to left and right and slow and fast signals. I am thankful to say I have never suffered the former fate, though the latter has sometimes cropped up at the most awkward moments during or before a race. A jockey who cannot pull up at the starting post when he is cantering down always comes in for a good deal of derision from his colleagues as he is carried unwillingly past them, and when a horse makes a habit of this irresponsible sort of *joie de vivre* he is best trotted, or even led, down to the post.

The Perfect Horseman's toes are always pointing forwards or upwards, his elbows are tucked in, and his back is straight. His impeccable style, and the way his mounts respond, are the visible proofs of the Perfect Horseman's qualities, but just as important is an inner and invisible asset, his intuitive knowledge of what his horse is about to do. A second's anticipation of a slip or a swerve is enough for the Perfect Horseman's balance to be elastically in the right place, and for his hands to be ready to give his mount all possible help in recovery. If there really were a Perfect Horseman, he would never fall off : but as far as I know, this paragon does not exist.

The Perfect Jockey is not unduly concerned with the theory, technique, and the higher points of style. His function is simply to win races.

His one indispensable quality is determination, for nothing but a ruthless, driving will to win will keep a man racing at all. Ruthless, that is to say, to himself, for the Perfect Jockey, though sticking to his rights, is fair and considerate to his opponents. He does not push other riders into the rails to break their legs, or flick his whip in their eyes, or kick their horses in the groin with his toe to un-balance them, or play any other of the sweet little tricks in the armoury of Dirty Dogs.

The Perfect Jockey sees every race as a battle of tactics, an engagement in which strategy should be based on a realistic view of his horse's capabilities and his position in the handicap, the racing habits of the rest of the field, the state of the going, and the probable blanks in the equipment of the other jockeys. He does not, however, follow his plan through blindly to a possibly bitter end, but changes and adapts it if the race does not develop as he expects. Brilliant seizing of an unexpected opening is his special strength, and when he comes to the last furlong or the last fence he is in the perfect place to make a winning effort with every spark of his genius for speed.

If there were in fact a Perfect Jockey, he would never lose a race by a short head. But, in considering such a near miss a failure on his part, it might be true to say that were he not a Perfect Jockey he would be much farther back, and be beaten by six lengths.

The backward seat is well displayed in those charming Victorian hunting prints where the stomachs of the galloping horses are almost touching the ground and the side-whiskered riders are sitting bolt upright with an air of sur-prise. It is still the natural seat, controlled or comfortable, of *haut école* riders and cowboys. Sixty years ago it was the only seat known in racing, but now its disadvantages have made it obsolete.

The rider's weight is in the wrong place, both for speed and for jumping, when he is sitting back in his saddle on the flat and lying on the horse's quarters in the air. The mis-placed weight affects a horse's efficiency over fences in three ways. First, and most obvious, it tends to force the hind legs down too soon so that they drag through the fence; and secondly, it acts as a back-wheel brake when the horse lands, so that he has to start away again hampered by a drag on his hindquarters. This can be clearly seen when inexperienced riders bring their mounts almost to a standstill on the landing side of a fence.

Thirdly, there is the matter of the length of rein. In leaning backwards a rider lets the reins run through his fingers almost down to the buckle. There are many times over fences when this position is the best way to counteract a horse's clumsy jump, but an inexpert jockey is apt to be unable to let the reins slip quickly enough, and the horse feels a jab in his mouth. If the rider is at all unbalanced and has difficulty in restoring himself to a more upright seat on landing, he hauls on the reins and the horse gets another jab.

The horse begins to expect this sudden and unpleasant pain and to avoid it refuses to stretch out his head. He no longer jumps freely; he 'props' into a fence and gets over it slowly, going up into the air and landing almost on all four feet, losing lengths, and indeed, the race. Many a good horse has been ruined like this, and it is very difficult, and often impossible, to restore any confidence if the damage has been going on during more than one or two races.

Drawings of races sixty years ago show the riders trying to avoid catching their horses in the mouth by stretching forward with one arm and lifting the other hand backwards off the reins into the position known as 'calling a cab'.

Although it is no longer the normal and recognized thing to do, 'calling a cab' is still occasionally seen when a jockey finds himself in difficulties over a fence. When it is a choice between lifting an arm or falling off, it is obvious which is better; and this choice sometimes presents itself when a horse ducks his head down suddenly as he lands. However, a rider in whom this habit is regularly observed is either a bad horseman, unfit, or scared.

If he is a bad horseman at twenty, there is hope; if at forty, not.

An unfit and tired rider, sitting like a sack in the saddle, is a dead weight on the horse's back. Towards the end of a race he has barely enough strength to control his own leaden-feeling limbs, and none at all for helping his mount. This sorry state of affairs is most often seen in amateurs who ride only three or four races a year and who rely solely on some spasmodic hacking to toughen them up.

A frightened jockey leans away from a jump because he is afraid of falling off, regardless of the fact that he would be just as safe if he sat up properly. Should a man find that a fear of falling is taking away all pleasure from his racing, he should not be unduly ashamed of what is after all a not illogical emotion, but he certainly ought to make a graceful exit at this point. If he goes on riding he will find his apprehensions growing stronger, and he will be an anxiety to his family and a danger to everyone else in a race. Worst of all he will be an object of pity in the sharp eyes of racegoers, who are so quick to spot a man afraid that they often overdo it.

One hears some odd things in the stands. At one time or another I have heard red-faced aggressive men with paunches, who looked as if they had never sat on even a mule in their life, talk through their pockets and loudly assert as a proven fact that (a) Fred Winter, (b) Tim Molony, (c) Dick Francis, or (d) any jockey who had come in last when backed by them, had lost his —— nerve, and it was a —— shame that they were allowed to go on riding, and lose a race that even a —— monkey could have won.

As far as I know, it is very rare indeed for a jockey who has been racing successfully for years suddenly to lose his nerve. On the contrary, mothers of National Hunt jockeys have been heard to remark that their sons are reckless to the point of insanity, and that one day they'll break their silly necks.

I am bound to admit that for the mothers of Fred Rimell, Dave Dick, and Tommy Cusack this would have been an accurate forecast : but they all survived.

*   *   *

In an emergency at racing speed the forward seat involves the danger of preceding one's mount over a fence, and the backward seat is apt to send a rider out by the back door. A middle way between these two extremes, although a typically British compromise, is not a weak or indecisive solution but the most sensible way to deal with British fences.

For me, in any case, the middle seat has always been the safest and most practical. Sitting lightly upright in the saddle, with the ankle, knee, and thigh joints all at right angles, is a basic, relaxed, and flexible position from which all things (including falling off) are possible. Bend the knees and lean forward and the weight moves over the horse's shoulders for easier galloping. Straighten the arms and lean back and one can adjust one's balance over a steep or misjudged jump.

'In the middle' is by far the best seat over big fences simply because it is so easily and safely altered to fit the circumstances : and whatever brilliant racing tactics a jockey may be capable of are quite useless if he is unable to stay in the saddle long enough to bring them off.

Whichever of the three styles he may favour, staying on when his mount jumps is every jockey's aim, and the way in which they meet a fence has everything to do with their continued partnership on the other side. The farther away from a fence a jockey can judge how his horse is meeting it, the more chance he has of jumping it well. I do not think it would be too much to say that the ability to judge this distance is one of the main things which distinguishes a good from a bad jockey. It is also, mercifully, something which can be learned with practice.

The best distance for a horse to be from an average four-foot-six plain fence when he takes off is about his own un-extended length. From here he clears the fence at the height of his spring, and lands at about the same distance from a fence as he took off.

In front of a regulation open ditch the best place to take off is exactly the same spot as for a plain fence. Putting it another way, one should take off at the same distance from the front bar of the ditch as the bar is from the ground. For instance, if the bar is eighteen inches from the ground, a jump from eighteen inches in front of it will clear the fence but not waste time and energy in making an unnecessarily large leap.

The same calculation is useful for clearing the water-jump. If the fence is three feet high, the maximum height allowed, a take-off three feet in front of it should safely land one on the other side of a ducking; provided, of course, that one is going fast enough.

A jockey's aim is to try to make every horse take off at the ideal place at every fence, but there is not a jockey on earth who can manage it, such is the cussedness of those horses which refuse to be helped.

What one does to put right a horse which is meeting a fence or a hurdle wrong depends altogether upon the sort of horse one is riding. On a good experienced jumper one can urge him, with knees and hands and voice, to lengthen his stride, go a little faster, and so reach approximately the right spot for taking off with enough momentum to withstand a mild collision with the top of the obstacle. Most horses will respond at once to such guidance from the saddle; and just how lost a horse may feel without it is clearly shown by loose horses, normally good jumpers, which approach a fence wrong and jump awkwardly where with a jockey they might have flown.

With beginners and weak-quartered animals the procedure is reversed. It is no use urging them to go faster for a few strides, because the extra speed will only fluster them and make their mistakes worse. Better to collect them and shorten their stride, so that again they reach the fence at a suitable place for taking off. Steadiness in their case pays as well as speed for fluent jumpers, and gives them a good chance of arriving safely on the landing side. It is easy to see, from watching them run, that green novices have little chance in their first few races of beating the old hands in their own class. They are left behind every time for speed over a fence if they meet it wrong.

Some experienced and intelligent but wilful horses insist upon looking after themselves, and it is undoubtedly best to leave them alone to get on with it. Instructions from the saddle only confuse a horse which prefers to correct his own approach to a fence, but it is a very odd feeling indeed to sit on a horse, know his stride is wrong, and sternly forbid oneself to do anything about it. One has to have great trust in one's mount's abilities, and enough control of oneself to sit still in the face of apparently approaching disaster; but if one knows the horse well, one realizes that letting him sort out his own difficulties is the best, and sometimes the only way, to get him first past the winning post.

It is never an outstanding pleasure to a competent jockey to ride such a horse, because he feels quite helpless after having resigned all initiative to the unreasoning creature beneath him. But a horse which puts himself right to jump is, needless to say, invaluable to an inexperienced rider.

Easily the worst type of horse is the one which refuses to be helped and is also incapable of looking after himself.

This sort of horse jumps adequately until he finds himself at the wrong distance from a fence for a satisfactory leap. No amount of squeezing from his jockey's legs, or any other encouragement, will get him to lengthen his stride, and he stubbornly pulls against a rein being shortened in an effort to collect him together. Straight on to the fence he goes in his pigheaded way, finding at the last second that a too early take-off will drop him down on to the top of the fence, and a too late one will bring him almost to a standstill in front of it. An almost perpendicular spring off his hocks is then the only way of getting over. Both methods are guaranteed to rid him of his jockey sooner or later.

Proper schooling teaches a horse a great deal about jumping, but after that his own nature dictates his permanent style.

The landing side of a fence also has its problems, and it is here that the state of the ground often has most effect on a horse's performance.

Mud, of course, is the downfall of many horses because

they cannot pull their feet out quickly enough to keep their balance. Ground which is soft on top and hard underneath, the result of a shower after drought, is extremely treacherous and slippery. Horses often slide down on to their bellies after as many as three or four strides away from a fence because they cannot gather themselves together on their crazily skating feet. It is a most frustrating sensation to feel one's mount floundering like this, but there is little one can do : an issue of athletes' spiked running shoes all round would not, I fear, meet with universal approval.

Paradoxically, extremely wet ground is easy to race on and tires horses less than sticky going. When a horse lands into watery ground his feet go deeply in, but the soft earth makes little resistance to his pulling them out again, and his speed is not checked. The holes he leaves are the nightmare of racecourse managers.

Worst going of all is dry, hard ground with only a thin covering of grass. Many horses refuse to take off from this, and none likes to land on it. The jar from its unyielding surface runs up the horse's forelegs, often making him shin-sore, and sometimes giving him a lasting dislike for racing in general.

The perfect going for steeplechasing is springy, well-drained turf, with thick grass cut to a length of two or three inches. Every horse likes to race on it, for it gives a good foothold for taking off and a sponge-rubber carpet for landing on.

When an owner says, 'My horse likes the hard,' or 'My horse revels in the mud,' he is really saying that if the going is not good, his horse is better equipped to deal with one of the two extremes, not that he positively prefers it. The only exceptions to this general rule are horses whose legs are very sensitive to any firmness in the ground, and who can race only in very soft going without laming themselves.

Even in good going, however, horses which have judged their fence and jumped well sometimes come to grief as they land. They knuckle over and go down on to their knees, having perhaps caught their toe in bumps or holes left by other horses. They jump very fast and cannot get their legs out in front of them quickly enough for their second stride. Or they swerve to avoid a fallen horse and their feet slip away sideways from under them.

One cannot make any sort of generalization about when a horse is likely to fall, though tiring animals under pressure are of course the most likely candidates. Clever jumpers seldom come down, but there are very few 'chasers which have never fallen in their racing life. Other horses make the same mistakes over and over again, and fall so often that one wonders why their owners persevere. Perhaps, though, they were encouraged by the performance of the late Lord Bicester's horse Senlac Hill.

Senlac Hill was a very long-backed, washy chestnut with four white socks, a white face and a flaxen mane and tail. In spite of hours of patient schooling he remained an ignorant and careless jumper, and because of his pale colour his antics were always clearly visible from the stands. Although he won a good race or two when he managed to complete a course, he became well known for the regularity of his disappearance at the open ditch. He not only did not pay these difficult fences the respect due to them, he often ignored them altogether. He used to put his forefeet straight into the ditch and somersault over the fence on to the ground, usually landing on top of his unfortunate jockey.

It was with some confidence, therefore, that I predicted my doom in the 1953 Grand National. The third fence is the first open ditch, and I arranged for several friends to be standing there with their hats off in suitable mourning, ready to pick up my remains. Bookmakers were offering fifty to one against Senlac Hill getting round, and said it was a crying shame to take the money.

Even Lord Bicester, whose dearest wish it was to win the great race, looked faintly apprehensive in the paddock, and instead of making his usual hopeful plans for meeting me afterwards in the winner's enclosure, told me just to 'Do the best you can, Dick.'

Finnure and Mariner's Log, two of Lord Bicester's horses

which set out with great chances, fell with me at the first fence. Senlac Hill took a good look at this big obstacle and mended his ways instantly. He actually jumped the third fence well. And on we went, over Becher's, the Canal Turn, Valentine's, the Chair and the water, and all round again. It was fantastic.

Only five of the thirty-one runners finished, and Senlac Hill was the last of them. He was some way behind, because he had not been able to combine speed with his new caution. Raymond Glendenning, commentating, reported his return among fallen horses cantering back, and said, 'Here is Senlac Hill coming in, but I am quite sure *he* has not finished the course.'

It is still reckoned among racing miracles that he did.

It was very unfortunate that shortly after the National he developed tendon trouble and finished his career at the early age of eight, for the only time I rode him afterwards he at last showed signs of correcting his previous mistakes.

Quite often a horse which is a jumping fiasco in its youth improves enormously as it grows older, and ugly ducklings fly through the air like swans. It is only when his horse has crashed his way consistently through two or three seasons that an owner must face the sad truth that he has bought or bred a permanent duck. It is usually worth while persisting with a horse for all that time if his sire or dam is good steeplechasing stock, for such animals often develop an ability to jump as they grow older.

The last part of one jump is the first stride towards the next. A horse should not be allowed to rest on his laurels when he has cleared an obstacle, and his jockey tries to help him make a quick getaway by pulling in the slack in the reins, pressing with his legs, and gathering him into a proper balance. When his mount has hit a fence the jockey often has quite a job to collect himself back into the saddle at all, and before he can urge the horse off again he has to be certain that he is going with it.

Making a serious mistake at a fence knocks the stuffing out of a horse and unbalances him badly for some strides afterwards, and he needs an easy few seconds to recover it. Occasionally one sees a horse fall several strides from a fence if his jockey, happening to have weathered the upset better, vigorously drives his mount on before the animal is ready. A more experienced horseman would feel the wavering beneath him and help his mount collect himself before he urged him forward.

The first stride away from the last fence is the beginning of riding a finish. As at every fence a smooth flowing jump, landing, and departure are the ideal movement. It is deeply depressing to come to the last fence with the race won, flounder over it, and see another horse, jumping well, sprint past while one is still trying to get one's mount going again. Thousands of races are won or lost at this fateful jump.

The aim of a jockey riding a finish is first to establish a steady rhythmic gallop, and then gradually to speed it up until the horse is going as fast as his lungs and legs will let him. A carelessly lifted whip, some paper blowing across the course, an unusual shadow, the smallest alarm during this final effort is enough to destroy it.

To achieve a long smooth winning run a jockey's hands are holding the reins lightly to give the horse his head, his legs are squeezing his mount forward, and with small scrubbing motions of his arms and wrists he sends at every stride a message of urgency to the horse's mouth.

In a very hard finish most jockeys use a whip to help them, though some horses are so rebellious to the stick that they throw up their heads and stop racing if their rider begins to swing one. Few jockeys beat their mounts or leave any marks on them, and a great deal of the apparently vicious whip-swinging one condemns from the stands barely touches the horse at all. Horses know that the whip is a signal for a final spurt, and it is rarely necessary to do more than swing it beside him so that he can see it out of the corner of his eye and tap him lightly down the shoulder to remind him to keep going. Australians tie white tassels to the end of their whips so that their horses can see them more clearly, but this custom is banned in Britain.

Owners influence the use of the whip made by their jockeys. Some refuse to allow their horses to be hit at all, most recognize that some gentle encouragement often turns a loser into a winner, and an unpleasant few do not care if the horse comes back bleeding as long as he is first.

Whether or not one makes an extreme effort to be second or third when one cannot win also depends entirely upon whose horse one is riding. Some owners have an each-way bet to save their main stake, and for them one must drive one's mount as hard as possible to gain a place. Others say that if their horse cannot possibly win they do not want him knocked about to come in third. In general, jockeys try to run into a place if they can, because the public deserves a fair run for its money, but it is not sensible or kind to exhaust an unfit horse in doing it.

Heavy going is apt to make the finish of a long race a graceless affair. Rhythm and speed are often conspicuously lacking as two or three weary horses plod along towards the post, labouring against the mud, and rolling from side to side because they are too tired to run straight. At this point their jockeys are often equally worn out, and have only enough strength left to ride a shadow of their usual finish. Three or four races like this in one afternoon severely tax a rider's stamina, for even on good going a hard finish needs a fit man.

The race to the post is the supreme test of jockeyship, and there is no doubt that the best finishing school is flat racing. All the National Hunt riders who attend it ride a strong finish. Fred Winter, Harry Sprague, John Gilbert, Dave Dick, Bryan Marshall, Martin Molony, George Slack, Josh Gifford, Bill Rees, and so many other good jockeys whose names could fill half a page were apprenticed on the flat because they were small and light at fifteen.

It is of comfort to the heavy brigade, however, to know that ex-amateurs Michael Scudamore, George Milburn, Alan Oughton, Tim Molony, Stan Mellor and Terry Biddle-combe have won more than enough races to prove that there are other ladders to climb.

The greatest advantage of learning to ride a finish as a
flat racer is that one gets plenty of practice. Close finishes
are not the rule in 'chasing, more common in hurdling, but
almost universal on the flat. Another advantage is the age
at which one starts. It is easier, I suppose, to learn any
physical skill at fifteen or sixteen than it is five years later;
and few amateurs, even at twenty-one, are riding horses good
enough to figure often in a fighting finish.

Riders may improve as time goes by, but the professional
flat-racing polish at the winning post is seldom acquired by
experience in National Hunt racing alone.

I discovered that I could ride a good finish on some
horses, but not on others. On those that went well for me I
found I could hold my own against Harry Sprague and
Fred Winter, but on mounts unresponsive to my brand of
persuasion I ruefully realized I was beaten.

Tim Molony developed an excellent finishing style which
depended mainly on his own great strength, and less on the
sort of finesse displayed by his younger brother. Tim was
also helped immensely by the racing system in Ireland, for
at the majority of Irish meetings, all through the year, one
event is a flat race for amateurs. He rode regularly in these
for three or four years until he became a professional in
1939.

I think the liquid force of a jockey in perfect harmony
with his mount as they race towards the winning post is a
joy to see. Every ripple of muscle in the horse's stretched
body finds an echo in the man on top. Like skiing and bil-
liards it looks easy from the sidelines, but it is quite a different
matter when one has to do it oneself, as I discovered the first
time I came into the straight with a winning chance.

I thought at that time that the best way for me to learn
to ride a finish was to study how the experts did it, but after
a while I found it was more instructive to watch the really
bad riders, and see what not to do.

The faults of beginners are glaringly obvious. Sometimes
one sees them, in their effort to move in rhythm with the
horse, swaying backwards when it should be forwards and

vice versa, like trying to swing with one's legs tucked under on the forward arc and stretched out on the backward. The result is the same : both swing and horse slow down.

Others frenziedly flap their elbows, as if a flying motion would propel them along faster, or flail with their whips as if they were beating a carpet. Most spectacular of all are the gentlemen who bounce up and down in the saddle while sitting upright. They seem to work on the principle that the harder one comes down the greater will be the next spring forward, like riding on a pogo stick.

Everyone realizes that a bad rider can make a thoroughbred look a cart-horse, but unless a horse is fleet of foot the Perfect Horseman and the Perfect Jockey rolled into one cannot regularly win races on him. The jockey is there to guide, help, drive, cajole, or even hoax his mount into the winner's enclosure, but he cannot go faster than the horse.

It is always a pleasure to ride a good horse, whatever the outcome of the race. There is, of course, more chance of winning if one's mount is intelligent and skilful, but if he is squarely beaten by a faster horse, the basic satisfaction of being on his back is not diminished.

I finished second in a race one day, and when I dismounted in the unsaddling enclosure I said, partly to please his owner, but mostly because it was true, 'Your horse gave me a lovely ride.'

'What has that got to do with it?' he answered sharply. 'You didn't win.'

I said nothing, but I thought a lot about it afterwards, and I realized that if I did not enjoy riding horses that do not win I could not be a jockey. No one could. It is a hard life in some ways, but the pleasures of race riding by far outweigh the knocks; and every jockey thinks the same, for if he did not, he would change to another job. No one can last long as a steeplechase jockey unless his heart is in it.

There are the rough horses to be taken with the smooth. By no means are all their steeds a delight to their riders, and it would be foolish to say that I looked forward to every race with the same degree of pleasure.

Stupid horses, for instance, are exasperating. They will not put themselves right before a fence, and they resist their jockeys' efforts to do it for them. They repeat their mistakes over and over again, and they never learn from experience; yet every time I went out to ride an animal like this, I felt an irrational hope that perhaps he would at last remember to take off when I asked him at a flight of hurdles, instead of rushing into them as usual, or to stop wasting his energy by fighting against his bit, and apply more of it to winning his race.

The horses I most enjoyed riding were those I had schooled at home, ridden in their novice races, and progressed with into handicaps. It is a great thing to feel a young horse develop under one's hands, and to watch his early promise mature into a successful career.

TEN

The Good Years

My association with Frank Cundell began, as so many pleasant things for me have done, on Bangor-on-Dee racecourse.

Frank did not go to the meeting, and I had not yet met him when I rode and won a race there on a horse he was training, but a few days afterwards Ken Cundell introduced us during a schooling session on the downs. Frank is Ken's second cousin, and they trained together for a few years after the war, until Ken moved over to Compton to start on his own.

Early in his life Frank was infected with the longing to ride in races, but he faced a drawback common to many young men similarly afflicted : no funds. With the clearness of thought and the ingenuity which are still two of his most outstanding qualities, Frank first became a veterinary surgeon, and then joined the Army. He had thus equipped himself with a permanent means of making a living, and transplanted himself into the heart of amateur steeplechasing country. An army officer can remain an amateur for ever, untroubled by the National Hunt Committee, who had breathed down Frank's neck more than once while he was racing as a veterinary student.

In 1934 he was sixth in the Grand National on Blue Peter III, but shortly after that the Army unfeelingly posted him to India. He consoled himself by serving as a stipendiary steward for three or four years at the Royal Western India Turf Club in Bombay. After the war he took up old threads at his late uncle Leonard Cundell's stables in Aston Tirrold, where he has been training with great success ever since.

Training steeplechasers is no easy job. I know little about

flat racing from the inside, and I was listening with interest one day to a man who has excelled as a trainer under both rules.

'Compared with jumping,' he said, 'the flat is dead easy. All you have to do is get the horse absolutely fit, run him against lower-class horses, and have a good bet on him. Enter him often, and pick your race. You can't lose. It's money for old rope.' He spoke with some authority that day : of his previous nineteen runners on the flat, fourteen had won.

'Why do you train mostly over the sticks, then?' I asked. 'More fun,' he said.

There must, I suppose, be a very good reason for a trainer to favour steeplechasing rather than 'the flat', and the fun and informality of the winter sport may well be it.

All trainers work and worry extremely hard : no forty-hour weeks for them. Up early in the morning to see their horses gallop, they then spend the day at the races looking after their own runners and studying the form of other peoples', and rush home afterwards to go round their stables to see to the well-being of all their charges. The endless paper work has still to be squeezed in somewhere : entries have to be made long in advance and the forfeit stages noted; corn, hay, straw have to be ordered, horse transport arranged, boxes at racecourse stables reserved; and the accounts have to be kept and the bills made up and sent out. Telephone calls and messages disturb his evenings, and at bedtime there is a last walk to be taken round the stables to make sure that all is well for the night.

All trainers worry at the same time that their horses may suffer some unforeseen harm that will undo in seconds the hard work of weeks : and when they have done their best, produced the horse fit, and still lost the race, they worry whether the owner is satisfied, or whether a horse-box will appear one morning to whisk the horse off to someone else's stables.

For all this nerve-racking labour one might expect trainers to be comfortably rewarded, but most of them confess that their only profit comes from well-judged wagers. They are, after all, closer to the horse's mouth than anyone else, but judging from the glum countenances of defeated trainers, those dumb creatures are prone to exaggerate their own chances.

The necessity to bet to live daunts me from starting to train now that I am no longer a jockey, for I am a hopeless gambler. I did not need the ban imposed on me by my jockey's licence to keep me away from 'the books' : in my case it is like telling a man who hates whisky not to drink it.

Hovering like little thunder clouds on the horizon are two distant threats to the peace and prosperity of trainers, the first infuriating but temporary, the second drastic and deadly, and both arising from dishonesty.

A few trainers, many owners, and thousands of racegoers are convinced that jockeys are continually being bribed to lose races. Let them be reassured that if any steeplechase jockey is seen 'stopping' a horse, word speedily goes round, and the rider in question finds that the number of horses he is asked to ride drops steeply. Although he might be paid a large sum for deliberately losing a race, he would lose also his reputation, many of his regular mounts, and perhaps even his licence.

Ironically, the very honesty of some jockeys has cost them their jobs, for in a few cases an owner has refused to employ a jockey again solely because the jockey did not lose a race when the owner told him to.

Only once was I offered a bribe not to win a race. I was staying with Douglas, who then trained at Bangor-on-Dee, and I was going to ride one of his horses the next day. The telephone rang, and Douglas came back from answering it grinning broadly.

'We have just been offered fifty pounds each not to win tomorrow,' he said.

'What did you say?' I asked.

'Told him to go to hell,' said Douglas.

A trainer may lose one race because he has had the misfortune to be swindled by his jockey, but if he ever employs that jockey again, or any other jockey known to be unreliable, he is taking a stupid risk. On the other hand, it is not always possible to see from the stands what difficulties a jockey may be in, and he may seem crooked while doing his best. 'Stopping' must be really flagrant to be proved.

The second threat to trainers is that of dope. This much discussed problem has not yet been satisfactorily solved, though the old rule automatically removing the licence from any trainer whose horse had been doped has been partially relaxed. If a trainer can show that he has taken stringent safety precautions, his licence may be safe.

There is no doubt that in the past innocent trainers suffered along with the guilty, and even now there is always the possibility of injustice. It is difficult, almost impossible, to prove whether or not a trainer doped his horse : he is really judged on the belief the inquiring authorities have in him.

Frank Cundell said once, 'If I go to one meeting, and send a horse to another, and someone there offers my stable-lad a hundred pounds for five minutes alone with my horse, I am held to be guilty if it is doped, and I stand to lose everything.'

In an effort to stop strangers tampering with horses in racecourse stables there is now a very strict watch kept at the gate, and all stable-lads have to show a passport folder with their photograph in it before they are allowed through. There is nothing, however, to prevent a stable-lad giving his charge a bucket of water to drink just before a race, and that alone is enough to slow most horses down.

It has always seemed nonsense to me that a trainer should dope his horse to lose. His whole life is devoted to the winning of races, and there is no point in his taking such risks to destroy his own work.

A horse that has been doped to win is an entirely different matter, for a good deal of special knowledge is necessary in this type of fraud. The doping must be done at exactly the right time, and no one but the trainer can be sure of having the opportunity.

I have twice ridden horses which I am certain were doped to win.

The first was a very uncomfortable experience. The horse was prancing about in the paddock on his hind legs, with a wildly rolling eye and foam at his mouth. He ran straight into the first hurdle blindly as if it were not there, and that was as far as I went. But the poor horse got to his feet and galloped for ten miles away from the course; a lucky thing for the trainer, because the horse was not found in time to be given a saliva test. This incident is a good example of the difficulty faced by the would-be doper. He has no ready-reckoner to tell him how much of any drug per pound of horse he must use to get the best results, and it is not a question one can ask publicly. My mount that day must have been given a treble dose.

The second horse was not so obviously pepped up, but the signs were there. It had changed stables only ten days before, and its new trainer did not realize when he engaged me that I had ridden it several times in the past. I knew it for a 'dog', a horse which hated racing, and as such it was the perfect subject for doping, for dope can make an unwilling horse race much faster than it would normally bother to, but it cannot do much good to a horse which is physically incapable of great speed.

The 'dog' had his day. He showed amazing energy and won easily. The next and only other time I rode him he was back to his old familiar undoped lazy self, started favourite, and trailed in almost last.

When I began to ride for Ken Cundell he had a great many jumpers and only a few runners on the flat, and Frank had nearly all flat racers. Three years later they had almost completely swapped over, and I imperceptibly changed the stable I was riding for. I still lived in the house which belonged to Ken, rode out with his horses, and did any odd jobs I could for him when he was away, but it was for Frank that I rode most races.

For Lord Bicester, Ken and Frank, I raced very happily

for three seasons, with varying degrees of good fortune, and an unwavering conviction that life was being good to me. I think I should have been content to have spent all my years of being a jockey in that modestly successful way, had there not lain ahead for me the heights and depths to which I have been since.

Although for many years I had been engaged to ride in the Cheltenham Gold Cup, I had never done so, because vagaries of the weather and frequent involuntary visits to Cheltenham Hospital had regularly hindered me, but in March 1953 I had no plans for the race. Lord Bicester's entry, Mariner's Log, was then trained in Ireland, and Pat Taaffe had come over with the horse to ride it in the Gold Cup; so there I was, fit for once to ride in the race, but expecting to watch it from the stands.

On the day before the race, however, Peter Cazalet, for whom I had not ridden before, asked me if I would ride Statecroft in the Gold Cup, as his regular jockey, Tony Grantham, had been hurt. I agreed with pleasure to do so, and next day went down to the parade ring wearing the pale-blue and white hooped colours of Mrs John White, sister of the late Lord Mildmay, who had owned and ridden the horse until his tragic drowning three years before.

It is usual for a jockey to go straight across to greet the owner and trainer of the horse as soon as he gets into the parade ring, but when I looked round for Mr Cazalet and Mrs White I saw they were talking to Their Majesties the Queen and the Queen Mother, who had come to see the racing that day and were watching the horses walk round. Lord Bicester saw my dilemma as I hovered on one foot, and beckoned me across to where he was standing with Pat Taaffe, not far from the Royal party.

In a moment Mr Cazalet was at my shoulder.

'Come along,' he said. 'I am going to introduce you to the Queen.'

I followed him over, bowed, shook hands with the Queen and the Queen Mother, and discovered how very awkward it is not to be able to take off one's hat in respect, when it is firmly tied on against the buffets of 'chasing.

It was a cold misty day, I remember, and the Queen was wearing a fur coat and a yellow scarf. We talked about Statecraft, and, Lord Bicester having joined us, about Mariner's Log also. Then Mr Cazalet helped me on to State-craft, and off we went to the start. Statecraft pulled a ten-don half-way through the race, and as I dismounted and walked back beside him, I had plenty of time to wonder at the coincidences which had led to my meeting the Queen and the Queen Mother, for I had no idea then that it was not the only time I should do so.

Six weeks later, however, Mr Cazalet asked me if I would ride regularly for him during the following season. It was a moment I have never forgotten. We were standing on the veranda outside the weighing-room at Sandown Park, and as he spoke I became aware of all that he was offering me. To ride for him meant riding the Royal horses : it meant as well that I had come to the last few rungs of my personal ladder; and even Sir Edmund Hillary, who at that very instant was climbing his way to immortality, could not have felt more on top of the world.

I said that I would have to ask Frank if he would agree to me partly leaving him, and that I had already renewed my agreement to ride for Lord Bicester, a contract that I would not break, even if I could. Frank and Ken, like George Owen years before, told me to go ahead, so I started the 1953–4 season riding for Lord Bicester and Mr Cazalet, and for Frank when neither of them needed me.

Peter Cazalet first started training as a pleasant hobby. He and two of his friends, Lord Mildmay and Mr E. C. Paget, owned a few horses and took great pleasure in riding in races, so all three of them kept their horses at Mr Cazalet's house, Fairlawne, in Kent, and employed a private trainer to look after them.

When he had ridden about sixty winners in seven seasons as an amateur jockey, Mr Cazalet took out a licence and began to train the horses himself. After the interruption of war his string grew larger, at first because more and more friends sent their horses to his stable, but later because other people saw what a resounding success he was having with them; and he very soon became one of the leading trainers.

From the start of the season everything went right.

Mr Cazalet had a number of young horses which won several novice races each, and Lord Bicester's horses as usual were running mostly in high-class three-mile handicap 'chases, so that they clashed far less than might be expected. The Cundell charges too seemed to fit neatly into the gaps, so that I rode a great many horses. And I won a great many races.

By Christmas I had won as many races as I had ever managed in a whole season before, and I was having one of those long runs of good luck which defy explanation. Not only did good horses win when they were expected to, in itself an unusual thing, but unknown quantities came galloping cheerfully in first, and unspectacular plodders took the lead when their potential conquerors fell. The weather was kind, the falls I had did not stop me riding, and all the time I was thinking, 'This luck can't last.'

But it did last.

After Christmas, with short breaks for bad weather, the run of luck went on, but it almost came to an end on Gold Cup day.

I was engaged to ride Mariner's Log for Lord Bicester, and I thought my excursion on Statecraft the year before would have broken the long series of mishaps which had formerly kept me out of the race. I was wrong. I rode Lochroe in a hurdle race earlier in the day, fell at the farthest hurdle, of course, and dislocated my left shoulder.

I retreated once again to the casualty department of Cheltenham Hospital, where the Casualty Sister took one look at Mary helping me through the door and said, 'What! Not you again!' I had seen her at least six times in the previous three years, and she suggested I might reasonably subscribe to a bed, so that it would always be ready for me.

On that day, however, I did not need a bed. My shoulder was speedily returned to its original design, I jumped into the taxi which Mary had telephoned for, and we went back to the racecourse as fast as the wheels could carry us. I was hoping very much to get there in time to see the finish of the Gold Cup, but as we walked into the paddock the last cheers were dying away, and the loud-speaker was announcing the result. Four Ten had won, and Mariner's Log was second.

The dislocation was a nuisance to me long afterwards, though after a day or two, when the stiffness had worn off, I forgot about it for months. At the end of the following December, however, I was riding a desperately hard finish in the Christmas hurdle, and just managing to keep my nose in front of Fred Winter up the straight at Kempton Park, when I felt my shoulder fall apart inside. The jerk it gave me was enough to upset the balance of my mount, so that we lost the race by a head instead of winning it. Needless to say, the owner of the horse was not very pleased, but his misery was nothing compared with mine, for this was a repeat performance of an old nightmare.

When I had been racing for only two years I dislocated my right shoulder and tore its moorings so badly that it was quite loose. My arm fell out of its socket at the slightest excuse, and although I could shrug it back into place, it happened several times in racing, and I felt that few trainers would employ a jockey who was likely to come to bits before their eyes.

Bill Tucker came to my rescue, took my shoulder to pieces and repaired the internal damage. From then on my right shoulder was as good as new, but I did not like the idea of repeating on my left one the painful operation and the four months climb back to strength.

In deep gloom, therefore, I made my way to Bill Tucker's clinic, expecting to hear the worst; but the damage was not as bad as I had feared.

He found that there was only one position in which my left arm was likely to dislocate by itself, and that was straight up. Apparently, in riding the hard finish at Kempton with my head down and my arms forward, I had literally flung my arm out. He suggested that if I wore a strap to remind me not to put my arm in that one position, I should be able to avoid another catastrophe.

After that I wore, under my racing colours, a strong band of webbing anchoring the top of my arm to my shoulder. I was not the only jockey who was held together, like a battered car, with bits of wire and string, for several others also are giving Nature a helping hand at weak spots.

At home, during my first season with Mr Cazalet, Mary and I had another engrossing interest. We were building a house.

Although we were very happy in Ken's house, and no one could have been a more generous landlord, we wanted to live in a house of our own, on land that belonged to us. A second son had been born to us, and I was already looking forward to their riding days, but we were enclosed by the village at Compton, and had nowhere to keep a pony. For two summers we had looked at houses for sale, without finding any to fall in love with.

In Ken's house, which was originally built in the year 1600, we had learned the drawbacks as well as the beauties of very old houses, with their wattle and daub walls, uneven floors, and absence of damp-courses. In the four years we were there Ken had had the whole roof retiled, the kitchen floor relaid, and an insecure chimney taken down, and we were discouraged by this from buying a house which might involve us in the same sort of upkeep. But we found that nearly every house for sale was old and damp, and those built within the last century were hideous; and finally we decided that if we were ever to have the sort of house we were looking for, we would have to build one ourselves.

For weeks the house was littered with little plans on pieces of squared graph paper, and Mary was often to be seen, tape-measure in hand, crawling round the furniture to see how much space it was going to need in its new home.

After a long search, we persuaded a farmer to sell us some land near the village of Blewbury, where the Berkshire Downs sweep gently towards the Thames Valley. We can see the long line of the hills to the south of us, and an Iron Age earthwork of giant steps lies to the east. It is a windy place, close enough to a road but surrounded by large open fields, with no trees near enough to stop the march of the sun round the windows; and it thoroughly satisfies the urges that Mary and I share for light, space and solitude.

It was alarming to see the lines we had casually drawn in pencil on our graph paper growing up solidly in bricks, and to realize that if we had made any mistakes it was now too late to rub them out. Nearly every Sunday we drove the ten miles from Compton to see how it was getting on, and stood shivering in the freezing wind looking at half-dug drains, half-built walls, and solid heaps of bricks, and trying to imagine ourselves living in the house that was rising from the muddy field.

Much too slowly to our impatient eyes the walls went up, the roof grew over the top like a monstrous spider's web of rafters, the tiles were laid, the glass was puttied into the windows, the plumbers, electricians, plasterers and painters came and went, and at long last, at the end of August, we moved in.

The adventure has turned out well, the house is still our pride and joy, and time has proved it comfortable and easy to live in. We have grown roots there which will soon be as impossible to pull up as the creeping weeds I battle with in the garden.

During my first season with Mr Cazalet, M'as-Tu-Vu was the only horse the Queen Mother had in training. He was not an outstanding horse, and he had no idea what to do when he found himself in front, but by clever placing on Mr Cazalet's part, and some care on mine not to bring him into the lead too soon, he managed to win three races, and was second or third in three others.

It was a great thrill for me to put on for the first time

the blue and buff stripes and black velvet cap of the Queen Mother's racing colours. I was not, of course, the first National Hunt jockey to wear them, for Tony Grantham and Bryan Marshall had both been riding for the Queen and the Queen Mother during the four years since Their Majesties had bought their first steeplechaser, Monaveen.

Except in the Grand National, when there are bunches of people standing all round the distant parts of the course, jockeys seldom hear any crowd noises from the time they leave the starting gate until after they have passed the winning post. Even the normal cheers and jeers from the stands at the end of a race fall on their ears as a distant echo, because they are altogether absorbed in their task and deaf to the outside world. So I was unprepared, the first time that M'as-Tu-Vu won when his owner was watching, for the tremendous roar which greeted my return in front. For a wild moment I thought something extraordinary must have happened behind me to cause such an outburst, but when I saw the hats flying up in the air I realized it was all for the Royal win. Of course I knew that the cheers each time were for the Queen Mother and her horse, and not for me, but nevertheless it was exciting to hear and be part of them. I often felt like joining in.

The Queen, the Queen Mother, and Princess Margaret all go to National Hunt races several times each season, and as I rode the Royal horses for some years, I naturally met them briefly many times. They take a keen interest in the sport and follow the results closely, and they are very well informed about horses and racing. Their comments are accurate, full of wit, and to the point, and whenever I was with them I had the comfort of knowing I should not be left, as I sometimes am, gasping and grasping for a sensible answer to a silly remark.

Steeplechasing is notorious for its filthy weather, but mud and rain do not interfere with Their Majesties' plans, and they visit the paddock to see the horses parade when many an ordinary person would stay in a warm shelter. One day at Lingfield I went out to ride in a heavy downpour. There were only three other runners; the parade ring was almost deserted, and only about six very hardy spectators were watching the horses walk round. But HM the Queen Mother was waiting under one of the big trees there to see her horse, and to give me her usual encouragement before I set off.

Their Majesties enjoy every part of racing. Sometimes they go across to the far side of the course in a Land Rover so they can see the start or be close to one of the jumps; often they stay after all the races are over to see any horses which may be being schooled over the course; and always they walk informally among the other race-goers when they go round to the saddling boxes to see the horses there, or down to the winner's enclosure after a race. Their real and undaunted interest in steeplechasing is a spur and a blessing to all of us engaged in it.

The course of the Royal horses has not always run smooth. It is as difficult for queens as for anyone else to buy a really good horse, and after Monaveen and Manicou disappeared from the scene, Queen Elizabeth the Queen Mother had some difficulty in finding anything worthy of bearing her colours.

M'as-Tu-Vu held the fort with smaller races until Double Star came along to win for her over and over again.

Devon Loch, however, was the greatest steeplechaser Her Majesty has ever owned. He was a big, fine, well-made gelding, with the intelligence and courage which distinguish a great horse from a merely strong one. But in my first year with the stable he was not in training, although he had run in the two previous seasons.

One day in February, when we had finished the morning's schooling programme in his park in Kent, Mr Cazalet said, 'Dick, have you heard about the International Steeplechase?'

'Yes,' I said.

'I have entered Campari and Rose Park,' he said. 'We will have to wait and see whether or not they will be accepted. If they are, will you go to ride one of them?'

I said I would be very pleased to. The International Steeplechase, as I very well knew, was a new invitation race that had been arranged by an American racecourse : any number of horses could be entered, but the Americans would choose the ones they thought most suitable, invite several each from England, Ireland, France, and other countries, and pay a good deal of their expenses.

Rose Park and Campari were both accepted two or three weeks later, and the half-incredulous hope of a voyage to the United States suddenly became a real possibility. There were still seven or eight weeks to pass before the race, and any of the thousand and one infuriating things which lame or upset a horse had plenty of time to happen, so that I was trying not to be too optimistic about the journey.

I expected to be going to ride Campari, because at that time I had never ridden Rose Park. Of all Mr Cazalet's charges, he was the one who had most often encountered Lord Bicester's horses, and from the beginning it had been decided that Bryan Marshall should continue to ride him in all his races. Bryan had been Mr Cazalet's retained jockey before me, but he had recently married and bought a house with some stables, ready to start training on his own account. Campari slipped and injured a hock in his next race, and my hopes faded a good deal. Bryan, however, decided he did not want to go to America, and when Mr Cazalet said he would find a second jockey at the course when he arrived, I was in the happy position of being certain to go even if only one of the horses was fit. As a trial outing I rode Rose Park in a race at Sandown, and he won it comfortably.

Mary and I were sure we should never again have such a wonderful opportunity of visiting the United States, so we decided that she should come with me, and that we should go by sea, stay over there for three weeks, and make it our summer holiday. We had no great dollar problems. My expenses for travel and a week's stay were to be paid for me, and I would be earning a fee in the International race; Mary's fare could be paid in England in sterling, and we were to stay for a while with friends.

Oddly enough, while I worried over every little bump suffered by Campari and Rose Park, it did not occur to me that I was the one who might be put out of action. I had been lucky for so long, except for the short lapse on Lochroe on Gold Cup day, that I had almost forgotten how suddenly the most cherished plans can break with a bone, and turn into disappointment and plaster of Paris.

By the beginning of April, I had ridden a great many more winners during the season than anyone else, and one half of my life's ambition was in sight. I did, in fact, finish that season as Champion Jockey; a most satisfying goal to reach and to remember.

April the tenth was such a glorious spring day that Mary and I took the whole family to Beaufort Hunt races. We lazed in the sun while the picnic lunch was demolished, talking about our coming voyage on the *Queen Elizabeth* less than three weeks ahead. Presently I changed into racing colours, waved to the children, and set off on Pondapatarri.

As I came to the last but one fence, easily in front, I was happily concentrating on getting home another winner to add to my score. And ten seconds later I lay on the ground unable to move.

Pondapatarri had fallen, but as so often happens, it was not he who had done the damage. I fell easily on my shoulder, but another horse jumping behind me tripped over Pondapatarri as he was struggling up, and as it fell over it kicked me in the back. It was the most sickening, frightening blow I have ever felt. I was instantly numb all over, and my muscles seemed to have all turned to jelly. I looked up at the high, white, puff-ball clouds in the blue sky and thought that the Atlantic would have to roll on without me.

Two first-aid men came up and looked at me, and after a while a doctor drove up.

'Can you wiggle your toes?' he said.

'Yes,' I said, moving them half an inch.

'Have you got pins and needles in your hands or feet?' he asked.

'No,' I said.

'Can you feel this?' He ran his hand along my thin racing boots, and down my arms.

'Yes,' I said. It was a great relief to both of us.

'Keep him flat on his back,' said the doctor to the first-aid men. 'He'll have to be X-rayed before he can get up.'

Bryan and Mary Marshall took our children home for us, and Mary came with me to a hospital in Bristol. By the time we got there the numbness was going from my limbs, and although from shoulders to stern I could still feel nothing, we began to wonder whether we might not see New York after all.

We had the usual long wait in the casualty department, this time complicated by its being seven o'clock on Saturday evening, long after the X-ray staff had gone away for a well-earned weekend. When at length the X-rays were taken the results were very hopeful.

'I can't see any break,' said the young casualty doctor, 'but that doesn't necessarily mean that there isn't one. We would have to take more pictures to be certain. Anyway, you can go home, and I'll get an ambulance to take you.'

He was a little taken aback to discover that 'home' was seventy miles away.

I usually recover very fast from my injuries, and this was no exception. A few days later I went up to London to see Bill Tucker, armed with the X-ray photographs the doctor had given me for the purpose. Another series of X-rays was taken, and this time the damage showed. One of my vertebrae was crushed and chipped, but not in a serious place, and it only needed rest, I was told, for it soon to be as good as new.

'Can I go to America a fortnight today,' I asked, 'and race in three weeks' time?'

Bill Tucker hesitated. 'You can,' he said at last, 'if you ride in a steel brace. We'll try to get one made. You'll have to wear a plaster jacket all the time now as well.'

I got him to relent about the plaster to the extent of agreeing that I could have a large brace made as well as the small one, and I was soon encased in an extra set of ribs and backbone made of metal and leather. I detest wearing plaster, partly because it weakens every muscle inside it, but mostly because it itches so badly; and as Mary does not knit we can never find anything long and pliable enough to scratch in the unget-at-able depths. The longest I have ever worn plaster was the four days it took to make my wide steel cummerbund.

Firmly buckled into my rib-cage, therefore, and very thankful to be going at all, I waddled with Mary up the gangplank of the *Queen Elizabeth* two weeks later.

ELEVEN

America

The *Queen Elizabeth*'s mooring ropes were flung out on to Pier 90 in New York at one o'clock exactly, and still swaying from our five days afloat, we watched the 2.15 race at Belmont Park racecourse on Long Island.

That first drive, in the car which met us after we had been whisked at high speed through the Customs, was in some ways the most interesting we took, for the quickest way to Long Island led through Harlem. The road was broad and lined with little stores blazing with neon lights in the sunshine, the people were coloured, and their clothes were brilliant. On every unbuilt-on space there was a Negro selling watermelons, and huge piles of these enormous green fruit were adorned with large and frank notices.

'Have a good belly-wash,' said one. 'Flush out your kidneys,' advised another. But we had not time to accept these entrancing invitations.

We were driven over the vast new Triborough Bridge and on to Long Island. We passed Idlewild (now Kennedy) airport, and travelled for a short way beside Long Island Sound, the stretch of water between Long Island and the mainland shore of Connecticut. The tremendous space everywhere made an immediate and lasting impression from our first hour in the country.

Long Island really is long. It stretches for a hundred and ten miles, but at no point is it more than thirty miles wide. At the western end there are the crowded New York City districts of Brooklyn and Queens, and at the east, the deserted, windswept stretches of sand at Montauk Point. In between lie little townships and communities, and comfortable country homes of wealthy people.

Mary and I spent more than half of our holiday on Long Island, exploring it from Oyster Bay on the north shore to Jones Beach on the south. Jones Beach stretches for so many miles that it is divided up into numbered areas, each with its own acres of car park behind it. There are no houses to be seen, and on the windy May morning we went there, very few people either. All along the deserted coast the Atlantic waves rolled up on to the quiet sand, and it was hard to imagine it as it must be in the summer, dotted black with hundreds of thousands of New Yorkers trying to escape the swamp-heat of their city.

On Long Island there are three racecourses to cater for New York's race-goers, Belmont, Jamaica, and Aqueduct, but Belmont Park was the only one we visited, for racing was centralized there during the whole of our stay.

The arrangement of racing fixtures is nothing at all like ours. Two- and three-day meetings on the big tracks are unknown : instead, the meetings go on continuously for six to ten weeks at the same track, before transferring to another one. A trainer may spend his summer months in racing near New York, and his winter in the south, in Florida, California, or Mexico City, for everyone moves from course to course with the racing fixtures. Horses, stable-lads, jockeys and trainers move *en masse* from one to the other, and hardly ever go home in between. It is almost possible for a trainer not to have permanent stables of his own, for the horses are all trained on the racecourses, and the downland gallops that we rely on here are a rarity.

At Belmont Park there are rows of stable buildings where each trainer is allotted as many boxes as he needs. They, like all the newer stables we saw during our visit, were built on the 'barn' plan. They consisted of two rows of boxes back to back standing inside a large barn, so that in wet or snowy weather the horses could be exercised indoors in their own stable by walking and trotting them round and round the long central block of boxes. Hay and other fodder for each trainer's horses can be stored on top of the boxes, easily accessible and sheltered by the all-covering roof of the barn.

In the racecourse stables a trainer's horses stay for the whole ten weeks of the meeting whether they are racing or not, looked after and fed by his own stable-lads, who live in blocks of living quarters near the stables and in rooms and lodging houses nearby.

The system has its advantages, for it cuts down travelling to a minimum, and the horses have no tiring journeys by horse-box just before they race. They live on the course, and gallop on it every morning, so it is all familiar to them when they are taken out to race, and it is unusual to see one sweating from nervousness. On the other hand, there is no privacy in that sort of training. At seven-thirty in the morning the car park near the stables is full, for owners, trainers, pressmen and punters have driven in to see the horses work on the practice track. Everyone has a stop-watch.

The trainers arrange the gallops with the lads who are to ride them. The horses start, the watches click; the horses pass the half-mile post, the watches click; the horses complete their gallop and pull up, the watches are consulted. Where everyone trains in the same conditions, and the state of the going on the sand tracks and cinder tracks is not affected by the weather, time is a sure indication of a horse's possibilities.

A trainer does not say to his lad, 'Go a good six furlongs half speed, well on the bit,' but instead, 'Go the first half-mile in sixty-five seconds, and the next quarter in twenty-eight, and then pull up.' And so acute is their judgement of speed that many of the 'work' jockeys can follow these orders to within half a second.

Close outside the racecourse entrance there are large snack bars and breakfast-rooms filled with the people who have been watching or riding the gallops. The air is full of the delicious smell of fresh coffee and only one topic is discussed : which horse worked how far in how many seconds.

Making a light and irreverent remark about the press one day I was surprised by the aghast faces turned towards me.

'Hush,' said a trainer, 'they may hear you.'

Remembering the banter the racing journalists exchange with jockeys in Britain, I said they were welcome to.

I was then given a serious warning that it was unwise to make disparaging comments about pressmen in the USA. They could use their power, I was told, to make me personally, and the British contingent in general, thoroughly unpopular with the New York racing public. The Americans themselves said they had always to smooth the press down and keep them sweet with deference and flattery, and only then would they write a fair report of a race.

Shocked, I launched into a glowing and accurate account of the friendliness of the race reporters at home. They never deliver too harsh or cruel a criticism, but are, on the contrary, quick to praise. One can be sure, also, that if one asks them not to print some particularly private fact that they may have learned by accident, they will not do so. They are the friends and advertising agency of the racing world, not the public informers and destroyers of reputation that their American counterparts were said to be. The existence of a benevolent and honest racing press, I began to see, was something which I had always ungenerously taken for granted.

Belmont Park is an attractive racecourse with little ornamental lakes and brilliant azaleas and other flowering shrubs in the centre. Inside the sand track where most of the flat races are run is a grass track, on which only two or three flat races are run each week. Hurdles are set up on this track for the occasional hurdle races, and next to it on the inside is the steeplechase course. From a distance the fences looked much the same as the ones we were used to at home, but when we got close to them we found that they were very softly built, so that horses could brush them without being checked in their stride. Steeplechases, in fact, are commonly known by the shorter and more descriptive term 'brush races'.

The enormous grandstands lie along one side of the track, and there are no spectators in the centre of the course.

Opposite the stands the most elaborate and informative Tote machine I have ever seen flashes second-to-second news across the course. Not only does this monster record the changing odds on each horse, but also the price forecast in the morning papers so that one can compare the two; and when the race starts, it lights up with the time in seconds taken by the leader to reach each quarter-mile post, the total time of the race, and the order of the horses as they pass the winning post. There were so many columns and squares of flickering figures that I never did track down the meaning of them all.

Every day except Saturday, when the races are usually all flat, there is one steeplechase in the day's programme of eight races, but the race the British, Irish and French horses were concerned in was something of an occasion, and it was given the week's most honoured position of being the sixth race on Saturday afternoon.

From their arrival on Tuesday or Wednesday the jockeys from Europe had a few days to get used to the unfamiliar conditions and a new set of rules.

We were absolutely astounded to learn that all jockeys have to be in the weighing-room before noon, when they are remanded in custody until they go out to ride, and that they may not see or speak to their trainers or owners during their imprisonment.

'Why can't we see the other races?' we asked.

'You can,' we were told, 'on television.'

We were shown the jockey's changing-room, which was furnished with easy chairs, writing-tables, and two large-screen television sets. On one the normal programmes blare away, and on the other, all afternoon, the jockeys see what is going on outside. This transmission is on a closed circuit for receivers on the racecourse only; there is one in the President's room, where Mary and I ate sandwiches one day and watched the racing from our armchairs.

'What on earth can we do between noon and the time for our race?' we asked. 'It's nearly four hours.'

'Have a Turkish bath,' said the American jockeys.

There were, we found, steam-rooms near the changing-room, and rooms with beds in where one could lie down and relax and get cool again. Dave Dick, who is six feet tall and fought a non-stop battle against his weight, spent most mornings in there.

The incarceration of jockeys is part of an extraordinarily thorough and as far as I could see completely successful plan to make racing straight. Working from the basic ignoble fact that some men will be dishonest if they are given any chance to be, the American racing authorities have set their minds to the problem of making rigged racing impossible.

Most of their attention, I regret to say, has been concentrated on the jockeys, for more than half the precautions can only be understood as springing from a belief that all jockeys are natural-born crooks. Locking the jockeys into the weighing-room is to save them from tempters and to prevent them from passing hot tips to punters.

In the United States jockeys are allowed to bet on their own mounts but not on any others; this is to encourage them to want to win.

When the jockeys are at length loosed to go out to ride, they do not stand in the parade ring talking to owners and trainers as they do in this country, but go straight to their horses, mount, and walk out on to the course. There is barely time to exchange a greeting, and certainly none for last-minute conspiracy.

On the track at each quarter-mile post an automatic camera swings in a slow arc and makes a film of its section of the race. After the race the pieces of film are collected from each camera and developed and projected in a very short time. The film can be run through in slow motion or stopped altogether, and if any jockey has been 'strangling' his horse or interfering with another rider it shows up unanswerably in black and white. These moving records are also watched a good deal by trainers who try to get from them helpful information about their horses so that they know what faults need correcting next time.

After a race every jockey, whether he is first or last, has

to weigh in, and he has no opportunity to shed or add a few pounds in secret on his way to the scales, for the weighing-in is done in the open air in a little enclosure beside the track and in full view of the stands. Before he may dismount every jockey must be given permission to do so : he raises his whip to ask it like a small boy in school, and may dismount only when nodded to. Then he returns to the weighing-room to be shut in until his next race.

To these deterrents against cheating there are added some incentives towards honest effort. The winner earns a double fee, and the second, third and fourth jockeys in every race get a considerable bonus too. The winning jockey is also legally entitled to ten per cent of the prize money for the race; as the prizes are large it is very worth while for any jockey to come in first, so that the bribe which might tempt him to lose when he could win would have to be enormous. In short, with a fortune to be won and a licence to be lost, the jockeys ride honest races.

The precautions to keep trainers on the straight and narrow path are just as careful. Every winner, for instance, is given a saliva test, so that any attempt at doping calls down instant doom.

Overnight declarations are the only ones accepted, and no trainer can slip in a surprise runner when the newspaper public is not looking.

To remove any jiggery-pokery in the running of two horses from one stable, all entries from one stable are bracketed together. It is no use a trainer deciding to run horse A to lose with a fashionable jockey while quietly winning with horse B at better odds with an apprentice, because horses A and B are inseparable on the Tote. On the race card they will be numbered 1 and 1A, not 1 and 2, so that whichever of the two is fancied by the punter, the Tote ticket will bear the number 1. If either horse 1 or 1A wins, holders of Tote tickets for 1 will be paid. Two horses belonging to the same owner but trained in different stables are also treated as one entry; and in this way there is nothing at all extra to be gained by winning with the unexpected one of a pair.

Although the morality of jockeys and trainers has been judged at its lowest, and their wings have been clipped, book-makers have been extinguished altogether. All betting is done on the Tote. There is no betting before the day of a race, private bookmaking is illegal, and in those days there was no off-the-course betting at all; but I imagine this has been one of the most disregarded pieces of legislation in America. Nevertheless, there is no 'starting price', no 'blower', and no betting in running.

Tote tickets are not cheap. The smallest amount the Tote at a big city track will accept for each of the win, second, and third place tickets is two dollars. The 'place' ticket only covers the first two horses, and the 'show' ticket pays a small return on the first three. For the equivalent of our 'each way' bet, an American, for his 'across the boards', buys a combination ticket for a minimum of six dollars. However, as in 1954 the stable-lads were paid sixty to eighty dollars a week, and the jockeys a basic fifty dollars a race, none of them found this scale of gambling at all dismaying.

Of every hundred dollars wagered on the Tote eighty-five are returned as winnings, eleven are paid in taxes, and four are retained by the racecourse.

Before we were granted a licence to ride in the race we had come for, the jockeys from Europe had to pass the thorough medical going-over which is compulsory for all American jockeys. Never did the Air Force pry so closely into the workings of heart, lungs, eyes, reflex nerves and abdominal organs as the racecourse doctor. We were told, as if it were any comfort, that after one such medical examination the doctor was able to say to one applicant, 'Sorry, you can't have a licence. You'll be dead in six months.' And he was.

However, it appeared that we were none of us in imminent danger of physical collapse.

The day of the race arrived, and with some anxiety we went out to ride in it. We had been warned by American friends that their native horses consistently covered two miles in under four minutes, and that ours took ten to twenty

seconds longer than theirs, for with true thoroughness the
newspapers had collected and published the times of the
European horses' races at home. It was no help to us either
to know that our horses had had a rough, long, and delayed
air journey lasting thirty-two hours only three days before
the race, and that none of the horses had eaten well since
their arrival. I was hoping all the same that my mount, Rose
Park, was going to produce the speed which had brought
him to the top as a two-mile 'chaser in England.

Alas for us all, our worst fears were justified. Rose Park
was a dead horse, and could not even keep up with the rest of
the field in the first mile. Campari fell in the second circuit,
but was not then lying in a winning position, and of all the
European horses Miss Dorothy Paget's Prince of Denmark,
with Dave Dick on board, covered himself with least confusion. He was fifth, in a field of thirteen.

Part, but only part, of the trouble was the difference in
the construction of the fences, for our horses did not realize
they could brush through them, and while we were wasting
time going up in the air over each obstacle, the American
horses were shooting by below us.

The Americans were almost as downcast by the failure of
our horses as we were, and hastened to find excuses for them
and to cheer us up.

Plans which had been made to run the horses again were
scrapped, and all of them except an Irish horse called In
View were flown home. In View ran in a steeplechase a week
later, and a week's rest and the experience he had gained in
the International Steeplechase stood him in good stead, for
he won.

At one of its autumn meetings each year the Cheltenham
Racecourse Company gives a dinner in honour of the last
season's Champion Jockey. Stewards, the National Hunt
Committee, racing officials, owners, trainers, jockeys and
pressmen all take pleasure in this occasion, and the only person who does not enjoy his dinner is the poor Champion in
question who has to make a speech after it.

In October 1954, as I shaved in the early evening before the dinner, and mumbled 'My Lords and Gentlemen' past the razor, I thought back over the events of the past year, and wondered at the great good fortune which had come my way.

In that year I had made a journey to the New World, built a house, and become Champion Jockey. Three dreams fulfilled, and all at once.

As I steered the razor carefully under my nose, I thought that there was really only one more thing that I passionately wanted to do.

I wanted to win the Grand National.

TWELVE

Devon Loch, 1956

A post-mortem one day may find the words 'Devon Loch' engraved on my heart, so everlasting an impression has that gallant animal made upon it; for there are few horses which have so engaged my affections, and no other has brought me such delight and such despair.

Devon Loch was an Irish-bred horse, and I first noticed him in October 1951 when he ran in his first race in England, a maiden hurdle at Nottingham. I saw a big, intelligent-looking, brown horse, young, but with the signs of developing strength.

In January 1952, when he was six, he ran at Hurst Park in his first novice 'chase, and showed form which was later seen to be very promising, for he was second to Mont Tremblant. He must have suffered some leg trouble then, because he did not run again until the following October; and after that one outing he strained a tendon in a foreleg, and missed two whole years of racing.

When I first rode him I found that he was as clever as he looked, and as I dismounted I said to Peter Cazalet, 'I would like to ride this horse in the National one day.' He smiled at my enthusiasm, because Devon Loch had hardly even started on the ladder of novice 'chases and handicap races that climbs to Aintree, where experience in jumping is the only passport to a round trip; but one could tell already that Devon Loch had the spring and the sense which would take him to the top.

He won his next race, the New Century Novices Steeplechase at Hurst Park. It had rained for days beforehand and the ground was a bog. In this race I rode Lochroe, who was also proving himself a brilliant novice, and who carried all the stable hopes that day; but he showed for the first time that his slender frame could not cope with wet sticky mud, and he finished in the middle of the field.

Bryan Marshall rode Devon Loch, and when he came triumphantly into the winner's enclosure, the Queen and the Queen Mother were waiting to congratulate him. Behind Bryan's answering smile lay a quick piece of stage management, for his teeth had been hurriedly given back to him on his way in by the stable-lad to whom he had entrusted them on his way out.

It is not safe to ride wearing false teeth, for they may easily be dislodged, lost, or even swallowed, and the hatchet-faced and grim look of many jockeys in the paddock is not due to a sour nature, but to their having left their smiles wrapped in a handkerchief in their coat pockets in the changing-room. Bryan understandably did not want to greet the Royal family in the parade ring with a large area of bare gums, and hit on the excellent plan of giving his teeth at the last moment to the man who was leading his horse out on to the course. Luckily I have not needed to copy him, for the teeth which survived Tulip have weathered all storms since; but every time I came back from a fall with blood on my face Mary's first question was always the same : 'Are your teeth still there?'

Devon Loch ran in three more races that season, and Bryan rode him each time. In November 1955 I partnered him again in a hurdle race, and shortly afterwards we won two steeplechases, one at Lingfield and one at Sandown. He ran without success in the George VI Chase; and he was third in the Mildmay Memorial while I was unwillingly nursing a few bruises in the sea air at Brighton.

The deep snows in Kent held back Devon Loch's spring training so that when he next ran, at the Cheltenham meeting early in March, he was not at the top of his form. When I reached the paddock Peter Cazalet was explaining this to Her Majesty the Queen.

'I'm afraid, Ma'am,' he said, 'that the horse may not be quite ready for this race today, for of course the Grand National is his real objective.'

'Yes,' Her Majesty said, smiling, 'but there's no harm in picking this one up on the way.'

But when the race started my hopes of winning disappeared. There were fourteen runners, and they set off at such a very fast pace that it was all Devon Loch could do to keep up, and he lay nearly last all round the first circuit. It was not until we were half-way round again and heading for home that the speed began to wear out some of the other runners, and Devon Loch moved past them, going tirelessly. He could not reach the front, however, and finished third to Kerstin and Armorial III, but he came racing up the hill at the end as if it would have been no trouble at all for him to go on round again.

The race, although it took place on the most testing course, was one of the fastest three-mile 'chases of the season, and was actually run at a greater speed than the average two-mile hurdle race. It was no wonder that many people comforted Peter Cazalet for not having won by saying, 'We have just seen the winner of the National in action.'

As for me, the yearly feeling of pleasure in looking forward to the National grew into a deep inner excitement. It made me laugh whenever I was asked about my chances, it made me sit smiling vacantly into space at home, it tugged at my nostrils and wrinkled up my eyes and quivered in my throat whenever the race was mentioned.

But there were still with me the fear that something would happen to stop me riding, and a sense of the responsibility that I was taking on. How appalling it would be if I fell off. What an anti-climax if we came to grief at the first fence.

Fifteen days before the National I cracked a collar-bone for the ninth time.

I was faced with a dilemma. If I admitted my collar-bone was cracked, no one would think me fit enough to ride Devon Loch, but I knew from experience that I would be. The ability of his body to absorb and disregard bangs and breaks is one of the things which make it possible for a man to be a steeplechase jockey, and because of his hard fitness the effect

his injuries have on him should not be judged by the effect
they would have on an average man. Jockeys feel the same
pain but it passes sooner, and except when the injury is
serious and complicated they heal faster, so that often they
know they are fit to ride when other people think they cannot possibly be.

Extraordinary thought it may seem, if a bone is cracked
again and again in the same place, and the ends are not
displaced, it causes less pain and inconvenience each time,
and mends more and more quickly. I could feel the cracked
ends grating together in my shoulder, but my arm was still
strong, and I decided that I would ride in a few more races
to see how things went.

The responsibility I owed to the Queen Mother, to Peter
Cazalet, to the stable, and indeed to the whole racing public,
weighed heavily on me, for no one would forgive me if I
threw away Devon Loch's chances by my own selfishness.

With elastic strapping on my shoulder I went on riding.
The bone mended and caused me no trouble, and five days
later I won a race at Lingfield, a race and a finish which
thoroughly tested its strength. All the way from the last
hurdle to the winning post I was engaged with Fred Winter
in a ding-dong battle, which my horse won by a neck. Fred
is such an artist at riding a finish that to have beaten him in
any circumstances would have been satisfying, and as things
were it was the best reassurance my troubled conscience
could have had.

In the next week I rode about six more races and another
winner, and when I went to Aintree I knew honestly and
without any doubt that I was absolutely fit.

From the moment, weeks before, that I had been told
definitely that I was to ride Devon Loch in the National,
I had been thinking out plans for the race. It is not really
very sensible to start off in any race without some idea of
what one is going to do, for a blind trust in luck is not on
the whole as useful as a calculated plan of campaign. Although the unexpected sometimes happens, it should not
happen *always*!

Working from the experience of the Cheltenham race, I thought that Devon Loch would lie towards the back of the field during the first mile, because that is usually the fastest part of the National, when everyone is trying to get to the front 'out of trouble'. A great hazard in the National is the number of fallen and loose horses which litter the fairway, and of course the nearer one is to the front the fewer horses there are to fall under one's feet; but the desire to be in the lead is the cause of half the grief. If there were only a thirty-mile-an-hour speed limit sign on the stretch to Becher's, far more horses would finish the course. The first fence is about a quarter of a mile from the start and many horses are going flat out by the time they get there, so it is no wonder that the toll of the first minute is heavy.

Two possible solutions would be to start the race nearer the first fence, or to put in an extra fence nearer the start. In either case the race would begin at a more sensible speed, but both present serious drawbacks.

If the start were nearer the first fence it would not, as it is now, be in full view of the stands, and the move would be very unpopular with everyone. And if another fence were built nearer the start it would have to be close to where the Melling Road crosses the course. Whenever the National course is used this wide road is covered with tan, which horses can gallop across without trouble; but one cannot take off from or land into tan, because it is soft and floun-dery and gives no foothold for jumping at racing pace. The problem is still unsolved, and every year the mad scramble goes on.

Although it seemed to be wise that Devon Loch should take things steadily at the beginning of the race, I remem-bered Finnure's sad fate and the way that good sense had led him straight into disaster. By the morning of the race I had ridden it in my imagination a dozen times, and had concluded that the risks of an unhurried start would have to be taken. With being so preoccupied in the morning and so despairing in the evening, it occurs to me now that I spoke very little the whole day.

The Queen, the Queen Mother, and Princess Margaret came to see their two horses run.

When I reached the parade ring before the race they were watching Devon Loch and M'as-Tu-Vu walk round, and after they had greeted me they said how well they thought both the horses were looking. It was agreed that Devon Loch had been very kindly handicapped with not too much weight, and that this was greatly in his favour.

Everyone was very hopeful, and though we talked calmly enough, there was a good deal of excitement in the air. Then Peter Cazalet helped me on to Devon Loch, and Arthur Freeman on to M'as-Tu-Vu, and with good wishes from the Royal party we walked out on to the course.

Even though the start was a good one, and there were, at twenty-nine, far fewer runners than usual, four horses came down at the first fence.

M'as-Tu-Vu went off in front, and Devon Loch jumped the first two in the middle of the field. But I soon found that he was not going to go slowly for the first mile, for he was striding out comfortably, and his leap at each fence gained him lengths. I have never ridden another horse like him. He cleared the formidable Aintree fences as easily as if they had been hurdles. He put himself right before every one of them, and he was so intelligent at the job that all I had to do was to ride him quietly and let him jump without fussing him.

Usually the National is more of a worry than a pleasure to anyone riding in it : Devon Loch made it a delight. Usually one is kicking one's horse along and taking risks to keep one's place : Devon Loch was going so easily that he had time to think what he was doing.

Over Becher's we went, round the Canal Turn, and over Valentine's, and two fences later had our only anxious moment. Domata, ridden by Derek Ancil, was just ahead of us on the inside, and as he came up to the open ditch he dived at it, and I could see he was going to fall. As he landed he rolled over on to the patch of ground where Devon Loch would have landed, but the great horse literally changed his direction in mid-air, side-stepped the sprawling Domata, and raced on without hesitation.

From then on I had the sort of run one dreams about. Horses which fell did so at a convenient distance, loose horses did not bother us, and Devon Loch's jumping got better and better. He cleared the Chair fence and the water-jump in front of the stands, and we went out into the country again lying sixth or seventh in a fairly closely bunched field. M'as-Tu-Vu was just behind us then, but three fences later he miscalculated the open ditch, and went no further.

During the next mile Devon Loch was gradually passing horse after horse by out-jumping them, and as we approached the Canal Turn we were lying second. Armorial III was in front, but Devon Loch was going so splendidly that there was no need for us to hurry.

Never before in the National had I held back a horse and said, 'Steady, boy.' Never had I felt such power in reserve, such confidence in my mount, such calm in my mind.

Armorial III fell at the fence after Valentine's, and Eagle Lodge took his place, but Devon Loch went past him a fence later, and, with three to jump, he put his nose in front. Amazingly, I was still holding Devon Loch back, and when I saw beside me that E.S.B., Ontray and Gentle Moya were being ridden hard, I was sure we were going to win.

Twenty yards from the last fence I could see that Devon Loch was meeting it perfectly, and he jumped it as stylishly as if it had been the first of thirty, instead of the last.

Well, I had my moment.

I know what it is like to win the National, even though I did not do it, and nothing that happened afterwards has clouded the memory of the seconds when Devon Loch went on to win. One might adapt an old saying to sum up my feelings exactly. Better to have won and lost, than never to have won at all.

An appalling minute after Devon Loch had fallen, I stood forlornly on the course looking for my whip. I had thrown it away from me in anger and anguish at the cruelty of fate; and now felt rather foolish having to pick it up again.

Devon Loch was being led back to his stable, and the
stragglers of the race were trotting in, and I took my time
over finding the whip, knowing that when I did I would
have to face the long walk back to the weighing-room and
the turned faces, the curious eyes, the unmanning sympathy
of the huge crowd. I wanted very much to be alone for a few
minutes to get my breath back, and as if he had read my
thoughts an ambulance driver came to my rescue.

'Hop in, mate,' he said, jerking his thumb at the ambulance.

So I hopped in, and he drove down through the people in
the paddock and stopped at the first-aid room, so that I
could go straight from there into the weighing-room without
having to push my way through the dense crowd round the
main door, and I was very grateful to him.

While I was slowly dressing and tying my tie Peter Cazalet
came into the changing-room.

'Dick,' he said, 'come along up to the Royal box. They
want to see you.'

We walked across and up the stairs together. Losing the
National like that was as disappointing to him as to anybody,
and in some ways worse, for twenty years before he had seen
Davy Jones break a rein and run out at the last fence with
the race in his pocket, and such dreadful luck should not
happen to any trainer twice.

It was quiet in the Royal box. It was as if the affectionate
cheers for Devon Loch which had died a long time ago in a
million throats all over Britain had cast a shadow of silence.
There was, after all, very little to be said. Their Majesties
tried to comfort me, and said what a beautiful race Devon
Loch had run; and in my turn I tried to say how desperately
sorry for their sake I was that we had not managed to cover
those last vital fifty yards.

Her Majesty the Queen Mother said resignedly, 'That's
racing, I suppose.' But she and the Queen were obviously
sorrowful and upset by what had happened.

Peter Cazalet came down again with me from the Royal

box, and we went over to the stables to see Devon Loch. He was munching some hay and being groomed, and apart from looking like a horse which has just had a hard race, there was nothing the matter with him. His intelligent head lifted as we went into his box, and I patted him while Peter Cazalet ran his hand down his legs to see if there was any heat or swelling in them, but they were cool and firm.

I stood close to Devon Loch and leaned my head against his neck. We were both tired. 'Oh, Devon Loch,' I was saying in my mind, 'Devon Loch, what happened? What happened?' If only he could have answered.

Peter Cazalet came back to the weighing-room with me, and with a few last sad words, we parted. Still a bit dazed and very unhappy, I collected Mary, and we drove with Father and my uncle back along the road we had travelled with such hope in the morning, to Douglas's house at Bangor-on-Dee. We hardly spoke a word the whole way.

The little house was full of children, ours and Douglas's, who were too young to understand what the lost race meant to us, and who met us with blunt and penetrating candour.

'The man on the wireless said Devon Loch sat down. Jolly silly sort of thing to do, wasn't it?'

'It's a pity you didn't win, Uncle Dick. I had a shilling on you and now I've lost it, and the stable-lads say their beer money's gone down the drain too.'

'Never mind, I expect you'll win a race next week.'

'Was the Queen cross, Daddy?'

And the youngest, just three, said nothing, but after he had seen the picture of Devon Loch's spread-eagled fall in the next day's newspapers, I found him playing behind the sofa, running and falling flat on his tummy and saying, 'I'm Devon Loch. Down I go, bump.'

All evening the telephone rang, and Douglas answered it. Mary and I went for a walk. There was a gentle wind blowing clouds slowly across the moon, and we walked along the country road towards the racecourse. Somewhere not far ahead in the shifting moonlight lay the rails and the now deserted fences of the course where I had ridden my first race and my first winner, where so much that was good had begun for me, and where I came now needing solace.

We reached a place where the River Dee runs close to the road and we stood beside a tree there, looking down into the black, sliding water.

'Do you feel like jumping in?' said Mary.

'It looks a bit too wet,' I said, 'and cold.'

The load of the day lifted suddenly and we laughed, yet nothing could for long ease our thoughts, and as we walked back in the wind and into our quiet room our sadness was still with us. Miserable and silent, we went to bed, but we could not sleep. To ourselves and to each other we were saying again and again, 'Why, why, why did it have to happen?' It still seemed unbelievable that it should have done so.

We went back to Berkshire the next day, and during the week which followed hundreds of letters arrived, many of them from strangers and from people who never go racing, and all kind and sympathetic. I had expected at least a few from cranks accusing me of driving my mount on to his knees from exhaustion, but I was pleased to find that the 'cruelty to horses at Aintree' brigade had not written a single abusive letter.

Four days after the National Her Majesty the Queen Mother went down to Fairlawne to see Devon Loch, and I went too, to ride him in the park, and to school Her Majesty's other horses. Devon Loch was looking very fit and well, and gave us no clue to the cause of his collapse, and as his Royal owner patted him I was sure she must have been wishing, as I had done, that he could tell us what had struck him down.

Her Majesty said she would like to see me again to talk about the race, and later sent a message asking me to go to Windsor.

She received me in a sunny room overlooking the mile-long, tree-bordered drive which stretches away into Windsor Great Park, and within the quiet solid walls of the Castle we talked of the excitement and the heartache that we had shared at Liverpool.

Before I went Her Majesty gave me a cheque and a silver cigarette box as a memento of the race that was so nearly won. It is a lovely box, and I am deeply honoured by the inscription on its lid. It means so much to me that I keep it safely in its case (and in the bank when I am away, burglars please note), and it will always hold more memories than cigarettes.

Over the finish of the 1956 Grand National there still hangs a gigantic question mark.

Much has been written, much discussed, many theories aired, many ideas exploded, but from all the fantastic explanations offered in a rush of journalistic blood to the head immediately after the race, four main possibilities emerge.

First, did Devon Loch have a heart attack? It has been suggested that when he was hard pressed a fault appeared in his pumping arrangements, and lack of oxygen in his lungs and head made him falter and stop. After some races he panted deeply and longer than one would expect, but this is normal with any horse when it is not fully fit, and after the National, when if this theory is correct one would expect to have seen him gasping for air, he did not blow unduly.

This theory also takes it for granted that Devon Loch was at the end of his strength when he collapsed. I cannot believe it. He was not going like a tired horse, rolling and staggering with effort, and I have ridden a lot of tired horses so I know the feel of them. He had jumped the last fence powerfully, and was almost sprinting away along the run-in : he had had an extraordinarily easy race all the way round, and was not having to fight hard in a close finish; and if he had completed the course he would have broken the time record for the race.

A seizure severe enough to stop him drastically in mid-stride would also, I think, have killed him. Yet five minutes later he was walking away as if nothing had happened. I have seen several horses have bad heart attacks when they were racing : they stagger for a few strides before they fall,

and they go down dead. Devon Loch did not stagger and he
recovered within minutes.

One cannot entirely rule out a constitutional weakness of
heart, but to me it does not seem at all probable.

The second explanation seems to be the one most widely
believed, and I am emphatically convinced it is not the true
one.

'A ghost jump,' said newspapers and newsreels in chorus.
'He tried to jump the water-jump which he saw out of the
corner of his eye.'

They printed strips of pictures and slow-motion bits of
film to prove it, and they did a good job on even the racing
world, which is half persuaded to believe them rather than
me.

The facts offered by the press to support their idea seem
reasonable at first glance. Devon Loch had had a hard race,
they said, and when he saw the wing of the water-jump on
his left he was too tired to realize that the jump itself was
not in front of him, so being a game-to-the-end horse he
tried to take off in a last-second reaction to the half sight of
the wing on the edge of his vision.

Also, said the press, he pricked his ears as a horse does
before he is going to jump, and a horse does not prick his
ears for nothing, especially after a long race. It seems to me
that if a horse has enough time and energy to prick its ears it
also has time and enough command of its senses to see what
is or what is not in front of it.

The press published pictures of Devon Loch with his hind
feet on the ground and his forelegs in the air. See him jump,
they said. But if a horse is galloping at thirty miles an hour
and his hind legs abruptly stop and drop, it is easy to see that
the sudden heavy drag behind will throw the forelegs into
the air like a see-saw. His former momentum was enough
after that to throw him forward through the air to land on
his belly, and this is what has been interpreted as an attempt
to jump.

A lot was made of the fact that the horse collapsed by the
wing of the water-jump. In fact, if he had been going to

jump the water-jump, Devon Loch would have taken another stride before he did so; no horse of such experience
would attempt to jump the water from outside the wings,
for he would know he could not do it.

The real answer to the ghost-jumpites is Devon Loch
himself. He was a horse of extreme intelligence. He was an
outstandingly brilliant jumper. He was not noticeably tired
and he was not being hard pressed. It is completely incon-
ceivable that such a horse in such circumstances should have
made such a shattering mistake. After all, he was used to
passing the wings of jumps beside him. A hundred and fifty
yards back he had passed the wing of the Chair fence without a flicker of emotion, and on other courses and in the
park at home he was well accustomed to galloping along
beside fences and hurdles without attempting to jump them.

Because I was on the horse and not watching I am sure
that the ghost-jump theory is wrong. When a horse is going
to jump he gathers the muscles of his hindquarters and tucks
his legs under him for the spring. However hurried he was,
no horse would attempt to jump without doing it, and if he
were very tired he would be more likely to run straight into
a fence and fall over it than to start to take off with his
weight all in the wrong place. I have ridden horses over
more than forty thousand fences in racing alone, not count-
ing hunting and show-jumping, and never has a horse intending to jump failed to gather himself together to take off.
The feeling is absolutely unmistakable. Devon Loch did not
try to jump.

The third theory is that Devon Loch suffered a sudden
and severe muscular spasm in his hindquarters, and the jolt
it gave him at the speed he was going was enough to throw
him down.

In the actual second of his fall I thought he had broken a
hind leg, for he collapsed from the back, but when I found
that he was unhurt, cramp seemed the only solution.

Very little is known about the physiology of cramp, and
the cause of the lightning spasm known as stitch in humans
is a complete mystery. Ordinary cramp in athletes usually

comes on after the end of a great physical effort, and is thought to be due to an excess of lactic acid in the muscles; in horses it is called 'setfast' and often lasts for six or seven hours. Obviously Devon Loch did not suffer from any prolonged cramp, for he was walking normally within two minutes of his fall, but a violent spasm equivalent to stitch seems a reasonable possibility.

If this sort of thing were at all common there would of course be no mystery, but veterinary opinion seems to be that it is so rare as to be almost unknown. On the other hand, soon after the race a retired huntsman told me that he used to ride a mare which did the same thing. She collapsed twice without warning in the hunting field while galloping, and once when trotting along a road; and after that he felt that she was more of a risk than a pleasure, and she was pensioned off.

Sudden cramp seems to be the most sensible, down-to-earth answer to the problem, but it does not explain why Devon Loch pricked his ears before he fell.

There is a fourth possibility. At first it may seem a fanciful and extravagant one, almost as alarming as the 'ghost jump'.

Devon Loch was galloping easily, he pricked his ears, and he fell for no visible reason in a peculiar way not seen before or since on a racecourse. If this was the only fall of its kind it is worth asking whether on this one occasion there was anything else which had never happened before. There was. It was the only time that a reigning sovereign had been at Liverpool cheering home a Royal winner of the Grand National.

Could there possibly be any connection of cause and effect in these two unique events? Sad and ironic though it may be, it is conceivable that it was simply and solely because he belonged to the Queen Mother that Devon Loch fell where and how he did.

From the last fence onwards the cheers which greeted us were tremendous and growing louder with every yard we went, and although I knew the reason for them, they may have been puzzling and confusing to my mount, who could not know that his owner was a queen.

In order to hear better what was going on he would make a horse's instinctive movement to do so, and into those newly pricked and sensitive ears fell a wave of sound of shattering intensity. The noise that to me was uplifting and magnificent may have been exceedingly frightening to Devon Loch. He may have tried to throw himself backwards away from it; he may have reacted to it in the same convulsive way as a human being jumps at a sudden loud noise, and a severe nervous jerk at such a stage in the race could certainly have been enough to smash the rhythm of his stride and bring him down.

The cheering was incredible. Everyone on the stands was yelling, and Raymond Glendenning's wireless commentary, though he was shouting into a microphone at the top of his voice, could scarcely be heard above the happy din going on about him. I have never in my life heard such a noise. It rolled and lapped around us, buffeting and glorious, the enthusiastic expression of love for the Royal Family and delight in seeing the Royal horse win. The tremendous noise was growing in volume with every second, and was being almost funnelled down from the stands on to the course. The weather records show that there was a light breeze blowing that day from behind the stands, and this must have carried the huge sound with it.

I remember how startled I was when I first heard the cheers for M'as-Tu-Vu at Lingfield, and they were a whisper compared with the enveloping roar at Liverpool; so I think one must seriously consider whether Devon Loch may not have been struck down by joy.

Heart failure, ghost jump, cramp, and a shock wave of sound may still not include the real cause of Devon Loch's fall, and in this tantalizing mystery there is no Sherlock Holmes to unravel its elementariness on the last page. What happened to Devon Loch is Devon Loch's secret, and I doubt if he even remembered it afterwards.

But what would have happened, I wonder, if we had

taken him to Aintree and galloped him along the straight to the winning post? Would he have noticed when he came to the fatal place? Would he have stopped and backed away from it with any show of distress, or even have fallen there again, or would he, as I certainly believe, have galloped on without faltering past the water-jump and past the un-attained winning post? Would he have heard the echo of the roar which met him there so long ago?

Devon Loch, a noble and courageous horse, will not be forgotten in racing history. Fifty years from now, about National time, newspaper articles will mention his tragedy as a curious event in a distant past. Octogenarians will sigh, 'I was there ...' The old photographs will be pulled out, and one's grandsons will wonder at the horse's sprawled legs, and perhaps smile at the old-fashioned clothes of the crowd.

And my fate? I know it already.

I heard one man say to another, a little while ago, 'Who did you say that was? Dick Francis? Oh, yes, he's the man who didn't win the National.'

What an epitaph!

CHAPTER THIRTEEN.

Afterwards, 1956–1981

Time never stands still, and neither for Devon Loch nor for me did life end with the 1956 Grand National. In the short term, the horse went out to grass for a summer holiday and his jockey picked himself up and got on with business as usual, and six months went by before the two of them were reunited on a racecourse.

Few fanfares attended the event. The time was an inconspicuous midweek afternoon at Nottingham at the end of October, and the race, two and a half miles over hurdles, was of such extreme unsuitability that a thumping failure could easily be explained away. The sparse crowd, cottoning unerringly to this ploy, kept their money in their pockets and let the Aintree flyer start at eight-to-one. The owner, not surprisingly, was not there to watch.

Well. Off went the field at two-mile-hurdle pace (usually faster than two-mile speeds on the flat), leaving Devon Loch well to the rear, insulted and surprised. He practically snorted. He tossed his head with displeasure and set off in pursuit. For me, feeling this thrusting enthusiasm, the biggest question was already answered : the old boy still did have his spirit and still did want to race, and I knew in view of that that it wouldn't really matter where he finished.

From Devon Loch's own angle things were much simpler. He was not aware that long-time 'chasers never re-find their speed over hurdles, or that two and a half miles is a sprinter's distance to a stayer, or that he was half-fit, first time out, and not expected to produce much against a better than useful field of nineteen which included the recent Cesarewitch winner Sandiacre. All he knew was that he had been offered a race, and that races were there to be won. Still near the back a mile from home he suddenly took hold of his bit and unmistakably announced that he was not out there running for nothing : so I too threw overboard his intended quiet return to the game and went for the lot. We passed bunches of incredulous jockeys all the way up the straight and won by two resounding lengths; and came back to more cries of 'Good heavens !' than 'Well done !'

I rode him in three more races. One was a winner – against National winner Early Mist at Sandown – and in the other two we came second. Of these undoubtedly the bitterest was the George VI on Boxing Day, because we were beaten by our stablemate Rose Park, who set off at a tearing gallop with Michael Scudamore, led all the way, and still had two lengths in hand at the winning post.

In January a fall put me out of action and Arthur Freeman rode Devon Loch in the Mildmay at Sandown. All went beautifully until three from home, where the horse, who had been leading, suddenly faltered and fell back, and limped slowly home. His tendon had given way again, and this time, from the racing point of view, hopelessly.

When he was patched up enough for an easier life, the Queen Mother gave him to Noel Murless, who used him as a lead horse for his two-year-olds at Newmarket. By early 1963 my old pal was seventeen and stumbling about with old age, and as the deep freeze of that winter compounded his miseries, it was thought kindest to put him down. It was sad to know he had gone. The end, for me, of an era.

Her Majesty's other horses brought home consoling numbers of winners as the years went by, and so far she has three times headed the owners' list of number of races won in one season.

Peter Cazalet never won his National, though he sent several horses to victory round the course in other races. In the 1972–3 season the Queen Mother's Inch Arran won the BP Chase in October and the Topham Trophy two days before the National, but these were the last great Cazalet successes at Aintree. The following May, Peter Cazalet died.

As for myself, the fall which stopped me riding Devon

Loch in his last race turned out to be my last, because I too never raced again. If Devon Loch had not broken down and had been fit for another try at Aintree, I would have gone with him, because given the chance, I could not have borne not to; but with him off the scene I was suddenly face to face with the agonizing choice that all sportsmen and athletes come to, which is between retiring before physical deterioration is obvious to all, or clinging on until kicked out.

It is tough at the top all right, and for jockeys as much as anyone. You have to prove with every ride that you are worth the fee, the trust, the horse. Prove you still have skill, strength and resolution. It is not enough to have confidence in yourself : you have to promote confidence in those who employ you. Some owners, not prepared to admit that their horse is simply too slow, always say that if the jockey had ridden differently he could have won; and however secure a jockey's status may seem he is always vulnerable to the public doubt which follows if he is 'jocked off' a good horse.

In my case, though I was not taken off many good horses, the warning signs were clear. The Cazalet owners, among the best and kindest in the world, began to refuse to let me ride their *bad* horses, and not just the dicey old jumpers, but the new, young, green ones. They did not want me to fall. They did not want me to hurt myself. Not on known tumblers. They did not want my fractures to be their fault.

Dear, dear good owners. That was the kiss of death. No jump jockey can afford not to ride the green, unpredictable youngsters, because those are the stars of tomorrow. And in their kindness, the owners could not and would not have removed the jockey who actually had ridden the risky early rides and put me up later for the 'safer' ones. I could see that I would inevitably be eased out, and not by doubt but by concern.

In truth I had not far to look for the cause of this killing kindness, because I knew perfectly well that my body was no longer mending as fast as it had. At thirty-six I was losing the power to shake off injury overnight, and after every bad fall that last season I tended to feel chilled and shaky, symptoms which had never troubled me before. However, as I had always vaguely thought of forty as a possible retiring date, I shrugged off these unwelcome signs of age and would not face their implications. And in fact I think I must have been riding as well as ever because the winners came without more effort than usual and I was leading the jockeys list most of the time.

At the end of December I won a strenuous hurdle race by a whisker in a hard finish and was really pleased by the kind things which were said, and during the next fortnight there were victories in a 'chase or two, and one on Crudwell at Leicester. Friday, 11 January I rode three races at New-bury; an also-ran, a second and a fall.

It didn't seem so bad when I hit the ground, even though several horses trampled over me. I stood up, had a ride back in a Land Rover, walked into the first-aid room and told the doctor I was fit to ride the next day. In the car going home the cold shakes appeared, and I began to feel ill. Once home things got rapidly and fairly terrifyingly worse. It seemed I had been kicked in the abdomen, and I spent the night lying on the bed, still clothed, in a series of fierce head-to-toe muscular spasms into which I went whenever I tried to undress. Doctors and specialists galloped to the res-cue but it was three days before anyone noticed I had broken my wrist. By then things in general were much better. Nothing internal had ruptured, and exactly eight days after the fall I was fully mobile with only a black-bruised stomach, mending metacarpals, and an anxiety to be back racing again within the month : and that was the day that Devon Loch broke down.

Lord Abergavenny, friend of the Queen Mother and later the Queen's representative at Ascot, had over several years given me helpful advice on many matters so that when he asked me to call at his flat one day in London I went without particularly wondering why.

What he said was stunning and simple, and was, in effect, 'Retire at the top.'

No one ever did, he said. Everyone always said they

would, but in the end they didn't. He thought it would be
best for me in the long run if I actually did. Maybe so, I said,
if I wanted to start training when I stopped riding, but I
didn't. All the same, he said.

In great depression I discussed his views with Mary and
we both saw him for another talk. His message was unchanged : go while it is a surprise to everyone, not a long-
awaited anti-climax. We both saw the good sense of this
course easily enough, but settling for it emotionally was
much harder. The decision itself took a heart-searching
fortnight but the miserable sense of loss lasted for months
and months.

Anyway, thanks to more advice and a little stage-manage-
ment, I had the luck to be able to say first on the TV
programme 'Sportsview' that I was hanging up the boots,
and Lord Abergavenny's hopeful predictions at once came
true, for within a fortnight I was offered three jobs.

One was that of official judge. This was a then unheard-of
position for an ex-professional jockey, and I accepted, feeling
that I had been paid a considerable compliment. I said,
however, that I would really prefer to be a starter, but was
told to wait a few years until I was not so much one of the
boys !

The second job was that of race commentator. I accepted
that too, and tried my hand at public race-reading at a
succession of meetings like Birmingham, Fontwell and Towcester. I found it hard work to learn the colours and horses
for every race, but at least twenty runners gave one plenty
to say. It was the two- and three-horse affairs which had me
most tongue-tied.

The third job offer was from the *Sunday Express.* They
would like four articles, they said, or perhaps a few more,
which would be written by their staff to appear under my
name. How about if I did them myself, I asked, and they
said OK, I could try.

During the early summer of 1956 an elderly lady called
Mrs Johnson went to tea with my mother; and this totally

ordinary and fortuitous afternoon altered the whole course of my life.

Mrs Johnson was accompanied by her son John, who was doing his good turn for the day by driving his aged parent. To pass the time while the two ladies chatted he wandered round the room looking at books and antiques and photographs: he had a pretty sharp eye, which my mother approved, as he had worked for some time for the Arts Council.

I was not there that day, but I've been told the same story identically by both sides. He stopped before a framed photograph of Devon Loch jumping the last fence in the National.

'How odd,' he said, 'that you should be interested in racing. And in that horse in particular.'

'My son rode it,' she said.

After a very surprised pause he said, 'Has he ever thought of writing the story of what really happened?'

'I'm sure he hasn't,' said my mother.

'Do you think,' he said, 'that he would be interested in a suggestion that he should?'

'I don't really know.'

'Well ... could you arrange that I meet him, to discuss it?'

Mother told me, and I met him. He said he was an authors' agent. He said he could get a ghost writer. He said how about it? And the consequence was, as the schoolroom game would put it, that I had a go myself.

I started the book – this book – in the summer of 1956, on a boat on the Norfolk Broads. During the autumn I was told that as professional jockeys were not allowed to appear in print the book could not be published, so my enthusiasm for what had turned out to be extremely hard and unfamiliar work diminished to a standstill. If I couldn't publish, why bother to write? But by February 1957, when I gave up racing, nearly two-thirds of the book was done. (The rules have been changed since then, and professional jockeys may now appear in print to their hearts' content.)

The one good thing about an autobiography as an introduction to writing is that at least you don't have to research the subject : the story is all there in your own head. I was lucky to have my first efforts published, as most writers fill copious waste-baskets before this happens, and I know that if this first book had been rejected everywhere I would never have written another. I was not filled with the burning zeal to write which survives three or four unpublished tomes and sets one to work on the fifth. I would have accepted at once that I should forget about writing and do something else.

But there we were. Michael Joseph, for whom I had ridden a few races, said he would publish the book when I'd finished it; and the *Sunday Express* printed the first article I wrote for them and said I could carry on with the others. I never really decided to be a writer. I just sort of drifted into it. For months, all through the summer of 1957, I looked upon the articles I was still producing weekly in the *Express* as only a stop-gap until I decided what to do for the rest of my life. The *Express* kept offering me a permanent job on the staff and I kept saying no, not realizing how many sports-writers would have jumped at it, but by the autumn the message had got through to my sluggish brain that I really did quite like what I was doing and that this was not some temporary marking of time, this was IT. In November I signed on the dotted line, and in December this book came out and sold out its first (small) printing in a week, and the exchange of saddle for pen was no longer a vague possibility but a fact.

Whatever I now know about writing I learnt from the discipline of working for a newspaper. There was small space allowed so that every word had to be worth it, and a deadline to be met so it was no good turning in a master-piece tomorrow. For most people, writing is hard work (though those who don't do it never believe it) and actually sitting down in front of the empty sheet of paper is some-thing to be put off whenever possible. Any publisher who gets work from me on time has the *Sunday Express*'s train-ing to thank.

My first year on the paper brought home to me a little forcibly that jockeys can earn more than journalists. The transition was softened a good deal by the proceeds from the book and also by something else particularly heart-warming, a retirement present given me by the whole racing fraternity. Peter Cazalet, Hugh Sumner, and the then Lord Bicester were the organizers and major contributors, but so many people sent gifts to the fund that it took me weeks to write and thank them. In all they collected a thousand pounds, which in 1957 was no mean sum. If it is of any interest to anyone who subscribed, I have never forgotten it (I still have the list of their names), and I appreciated the generosity with which the gift was given as much as the money itself.

Looking ahead, though, it was clear that the drop in income meant either changing the way we had grown used to living, or spending all our savings, or earning more money. We did the first to some extent and tried not to do the second, but the most sensible seemed the third. So I regret to say it was not inspiration which prompted me to start another book, but the threadbare state of a carpet and a rattle in my car : I thought that if a novel could cover those few expenses the labour might be worth it. I underestimated twice. Writing a novel proved to be the hardest, most self-analysing task I had ever attempted, far worse than an autobiography : and its rewards were greater than I expected.

The book, called *Dead Cert*, was accepted by the firm of Michael Joseph Ltd (Michael himself having died) who published it in January 1962, and on publication day I received a preliminary cheque for three hundred pounds which felt like turning from amateur to professional all over again.

Encouraged, I started anew, and *Nerve* was published two years later. Since then I have written one novel a year, and hope to continue for as long as anyone wants to read them. They have bought a new carpet or two by now, and a car or so, and of course a good deal more. I have been very lucky indeed in the rewards, but I still find the writing itself to be grindingly hard, and I approach Chapter One each year with deeper foreboding than I ever faced Becher's.

The process of producing fiction is a mystery which I still do not understand. Indeed, as the years go by I understand it less and less, and I am constantly afraid that one day I will lose the knack of it and produce discord, like a pianist forgetting where to find middle C.

People often ask me where I get ideas from, and the true answer is that I don't really know. They ask me how or why I write the way I do, and the answer is that I don't know that either. It seems to me now that one can't choose these things and that one has very little control over them. Jane Austen couldn't have written Charles Dickens, nor Charles Dickens, Jane Austen; and although I'm not in that league I couldn't write for instance Desmond Bagley nor he me with any sort of credibility. Books write authors as much as authors write books.

Touching the actual technique of writing, I listen in a slight daze to people talking knowledgeably of 'first drafts' and 'second drafts', because when I began to write I didn't know such things existed. I also didn't know that book authors commonly have 'editors', publishers' assistants who tidy the prose and suggest changes of content: I thought that a book as first written was what got (or didn't get) published, and I wrote accordingly. The first shot had to be the best I could do.

I still write that way. My 'first draft' is *it*. I can't rewrite to any extent: I've tried once or twice, but I haven't the mental stamina and I feel all the time that although what I'm attempting may be different it won't be *better* and may very well be worse, because my heart isn't in it. Publishers' editors have mournfully bowed to this state of affairs and resignedly ask only for a single word to be changed here or there, or for something obscure to be explained.

When I write any one sentence, I think first of all of what I want it to say. Then I think of a way of saying it. Usually at that point I write it down (in longhand, in pencil, in an exercise book) but if it seems the form my thought has taken is a bit dull or pompous I just sit and wait, and after a while a new shape of words drifts into my head, and I write that down instead. Sometimes I rub bits out and try again, but once the sentence looks all right on paper I go on to the next one and repeat the process, and so on. It's all pretty slow, as one sentence can sometimes take half an hour.

On the following morning I read yesterday's efforts and if they still look all right I go on from there. If they don't, I may despair that my work isn't good enough but all the same I don't often alter it except to add a word or two or perhaps insert a whole new sentence. When I've done a couple of chapters I type them out and it is this typescript when finished which goes to the printer.

I start consequently at Chapter 1, page 1, and plod on to the end; and although by page 1 I have a fair idea of what the book is going to be about in general, I never know exactly what is going to happen. The story grows while I write it.

I expect a great many authors work this way, if not most; and it is this gradual evolution of sentences, images, thoughts and plot patterns that I used to take for granted but now find increasingly mysterious.

Thanks to John Johnson's efforts, and more recently to those of his associate and successor, Andrew Hewson, the books have spread around the world in widening ripples, turning up in many languages, including for instance Norwegian, Czechoslovakian and Japanese. They've been read as serials and been dramatized into plays for radio; been recorded on cassettes and printed in large type for poor eyes; they've been abridged and digested and also simplified for adults just learning to read.

It would be unnatural not to take pleasure in all this and I am in fact vain enough to get a kick out of seeing the books in airport bookstalls from Paris to Los Angeles and in finding them in odd places like a village store-cum-restaurant in the back of beyond in Africa where we stopped for breakfast one morning. When Pan Books advertised *Bonecrack* on the front of the London buses (during May 1973) I stood in Oxford Street watching them go by with an absolutely fatuous smile.

Over the years the books have collected some much prized awards – first a Silver Dagger (runner-up, best crime novel, British awards) for *For Kicks* in 1965, then in 1970 in America the Edgar Allan Poe award for the best mystery of the year for *Forfeit*.

In 1980–81 to my surprise and delight the one book, *Whip Hand*, took both top awards, the Gold Dagger in Britain and the 'Edgar' in America. People may think I am blasé about these votes of confidence, but I absolutely am not: I am quite humbly proud of the honour of being given them.

Although film options have been taken out from time to time on most of the books, it seems that the stories are difficult to translate. Only one, *Dead Cert*, has so far reached the big screen, and in spite of its marvellous action scenes it made little impact at the box office. The Russians, incidentally, made their own *Dead Cert* movie to show on Moscow television; it lasted three hours in all and was shown twice, so that when I went to Moscow in 1977 I found that almost everyone had seen it, although I didn't until then know it had been made. The Russian television people invited Mary and me to see clips of it privately, and we found it delightful, even though we couldn't understand a word that was said and guessed the standard of the racing would give our own Jockey Club a fit.

Television indeed seems to suit the stories fairly well and I was very pleased when Yorkshire Television used *Odds Against* as the basis for a series of six episodes, shown under the umbrella title of *The Racing Game*. The success of this short series, due almost entirely to the skills of producer Jacky Stoller and actor Mike Gwilym, has had a direct effect on my life in many ways, not least in America, where the films were shown and repeated on public service television, coast to coast. Sales of the books themselves more than doubled in America in the year that *The Racing Game* appeared, hoisting me into a bracket there that I had not earlier achieved.

To Mike Gwilym also I owe the existence of the double award-winner, *Whip Hand*, since it was because the Royal Shakespeare Company actor so incredibly matched my concept of Sid Halley, chief character of *Odds Against*, that I became interested in writing a second book about the same man. Sid Halley, in *Odds Against*, lost his left hand, and in *Whip Hand* I set out to explore the mental difficulties of someone coming to terms with such a loss. In the event it proved a most disturbing book to write, a psychological wringer which gave me insomnia for months.

In publishing circles they talk about authors being 'on a plateau'. They mean that an author who has had a little success will remain on that level for a while. Then something, perhaps a better-than-usual book or perhaps a quirk of publicity, will raise the sales to a new level – to a new plateau, where things will again remain level for a while. A further boost may achieve a new higher plateau, and so on until one presumably falls off the top of the mountain because there's nowhere else to go.

A 'plateau' can last from a few years to a lifetime. I've discernibly reached three plateaux so far, each lasting for a good long while. *The Racing Game* and *Whip Hand* took me to the third plateau, where I stand at this time of writing: and the view from here is great. If to be fulfilled as a writer is to be read, then I can never complain.

On the personal front the years have brought more comforts than sadnesses, more cement than dissolution. My first-sight wife puts up with me still and has become my chief and indispensable researcher. As with so much else in our lives, what later came to seem full-time and inevitable began casually, in this case with a few notes about quartz and gem stones gathered from the tomes of Oxford's public library, used as background in *Odds Against*.

A year later we flew to Italy on a horse-transport plane, with me working my passage helping with the horses themselves and Mary taking general notes and photographs. We set off from Gatwick at 6 a.m., flew in an old unpressurized DC4 to Milan, spent three hours on the ground and returned to England, loading and unloading eight horses at each end. By a late bedtime we were hopelessly exhausted – but we had the whole basis of *Flying Finish*.

A little later, for that same book, we went to Oxford airport to gather some up-to-date information about civilian flying and light aircraft, as my own RAF knowledge was not applicable. We asked so many questions that the instructors suggested I took up flying again myself to find out the answers. Because of my newspaper work I said I didn't have time. Send your wife, they answered jokingly; and she went.

Until the day she took her first lesson she had literally never touched a small aeroplane. She had no real desire to fly and intended to go up two or three times only, just for as long as there were research questions to ask.

'Thanks,' I said, after her third flight. 'That's fine. You needn't bother any more.'

'Er, um,' she said. 'I like it. I think I'll just have two or three more lessons.'

After those she thought she might just as well go on until she'd flown solo. 'Just for the satisfaction.'

The satisfaction lasted for four quiet months. Then she pensively said, 'I think I might go back and get my licence . . .' and that time there was no stopping. She flew in all for eleven years, gaining a much cherished Instrument Rating which enabled her to fly on the airways. We owned at one time three small aircraft, two leased as an investment to the Oxford Air School and one which Mary flew herself and which we also operated (with commercial pilots) as an air-taxi, chiefly ferrying owners, trainers and jockeys to the races.

The book *Rat Race* stemmed entirely from our air-taxi firm, which flourished later under another ownership but still bears the name we gave it, Merlix Air, a name made up from half of Merrick and half of Felix (our sons; wholly sentimental). Mary herself wrote a book on how to fly aeroplanes, at first called *A Beginner's Guide to Flying* but now revised and brought up to date as *Flying Start*.

In the course of research for *In the Frame* she learnt to paint in oils, and because of *Reflex* became a semi-professional photographer with a darkroom in the bathroom. *Twice Shy* found her learning how to write computer programmes. For *Smokescreen* she went down a gold mine and for *Whip Hand* we both went up in a hot-air balloon. However, if I want to write about scuba diving round sunken wrecks, she says I'll have to do it on my own.

Our two little boys are now grown men with lives, houses and wives of their own. Merrick inherited the racing blood and trains both flat racers and jumpers in the village of Lambourn. Felix, a natural-born pilot, would have liked a career in the RAF or in civilian flying, but a hip operation which he underwent in childhood deterred the institutions from accepting him. With a degree in physics behind him he turned to schoolmastering instead, and is to me a highly useful source of information about bombs, guns and general scientific mayhem.

Both boys married great girls, and now we have several much-loved grandchildren to give an extra dimension to our lives. The 1954 house though modified is still home for Mary and me, and probably always will be. From there we see the new generations rising, and we are both aware that in all important ways we are deeply and undeservedly fortunate.

There have of course been disappointments, anxieties and griefs, as there are in every life. I feel particularly keenly the loss of my publisher, Anthea Joseph, who died of cancer in her mid-fifties in January 1981. Left the young widow of Michael Joseph, she was promoted chief editorial director and then chairman of the firm, seeing it grow under her expert influence into one of the greatest of publishing houses, and becoming herself throughout the book-world exceptionally admired and loved. I was privileged to read a poem for her at her memorial service, a sad requiem to a close friendship and business relationship which had lasted twenty years.

In 1973 after sixteen years I gave up my column in the *Sunday Express* and, although it had been an absorbing, rewarding occupation, I retired that time without any of the earlier awful feeling of amputation. The second time I was not being irrevocably severed from a job I loved, but moving on to wider horizons.

Since then Mary and I have travelled a good deal and met fascinating people of all sorts all round the world. We've been wherever the chances arose – such as to America, Australia, New Zealand, Holland and Norway for book-promotion tours, to South Africa and to Canada to judge hunters in international horse shows, to race meetings in Czechoslovakia and sophisticated Singapore and odd out-of-the-way places where the grandstands were a grassy bank. I've found that moving everywhere simultaneously in two different worlds – horses and books – has given me perhaps wider understandings of humanity than either might have done on its own.

Looking back to the 1956 Grand National, so much that has happened since that day seems incredible. One is forced to wonder how much would have been the same if Devon Loch had won that race; and in honesty I think I owe more to his collapse than I might have to his victory.

I was a jockey for a little over ten years. To be precise, there were nine years and eight months between my first win on Wrenbury Tiger and my last on Crudwell: and despite all the satisfactions that have come my way since, those years in retrospect were the special ones. The first growth; the true vintage.

The best years of my life.

Index

Abergavenny, Lord, 209, 210
Aintree course, 66–7, 120–33,
    136, 142, 207, 208
Alexandrina, 121
Amateur Jockeys List, 55
Ancil, Derek, 195
Anthony, Ivor, 33
Anthony, Jack, 22
Armorial III, 192, 196
Ascot course, 136, 209

Balding, Gerald, 73
Ballymonis, 27–8
Beeby, George, 65, 72, 114
Bicester, Lord, 62, 64–6, 68–73,
    113–15, 116–20, 141, 156,
    167–70, 176, 213
Biddlecombe, Terry, 159
Bissil, Jack, 52
Black, Dick, 54, 106, 117
Blitz Boy, 54
Blue Peter III, 163
Bluff King, 116–17
Bonner, Harry, 62
Boyd Rochfort, Capt, 120
Brabazon, Aubrey, 118
Bullingdon, 67

Campari, 175–77, 188
Cazalet, Peter, 135, 168–70,
    172, 173, 175–6, 190, 191–3,
    195, 197–8, 207, 213
Cheltenham course, 140–2
Churchtown, 122

Cloncarrig, 116
Coloured School Boy, 118
Cooper, Mrs D. M., 121
Corbett, Atty, 101
Cottage Rake, 116, 118
Cromwell, 66
Crudwell, 113, 120–3, 128, 138,
    209, 220
Cundell, Frank, 121, 163, 166,
    169–70
Cundell, Ken, 72–3, 76, 167,
    169–70, 172
Cundell, Leonard, 163
Cusack, Tommy, 151

Davy Jones, 66, 197
Dennis, Victor Dyke, 45, 56,
    63–4, 109
Dennis, Wenfra, 56, 63
Devon and Exeter course,
    138
Devon Loch, 11, 72, 113,
    122–3, 175, 190–205, 206–7,
    208, 209, 211, 220
Dick, Dave, 97, 106, 120, 151,
    159, 185, 188
Dixon, Oliver, 35
Domata, 138, 195
Doncaster course, 135–6, 137
Double Star, 175
Dowdeswell, Jack, 81

Eagle Lodge, 196
Early Mist, 120, 207

Elizabeth II, H.M. Queen, 20, 21, 168–9, 174–5, 191, 195, 197–8, 209

Elizabeth the Queen Mother, H.M. Queen, 11, 168–9, 174–5, 191–3, 195, 197, 203, 207, 209

E.S.B., 11, 136, 196

Evans, Gwynne, 32

Fighting Line, 72, 81

Finnure, 113, 117–19, 138, 156, 194

Fontwell Park course, 136

Four Ten, 88–9, 171

Francis, Dick:
advice given by other jockeys, 53
ambition to become a jockey, 29, 30, 32, 46–7
America, 180–9
becomes professional, 58–9
becomes a writer, 211–14
begins to ride for Lord Bicester, 62
begins to ride for Ken Cundell, 72
begins to ride for Frank Cundell, 121, 163
begins to ride for Peter Cazalet, 168
begins to ride royal horses, 173–4
books' sales and success, 215
courses, 124–42
Devon Loch's Grand National, 11, 190–1; theories on, 199–205
early life, 13–28
Embrook Stables, 33–5, 44
favourite horses, 113–23
first Grand National, 69–70

first meets the royal owners, 168–9
first point-to-point, 45
first race, 50–2
hunting, 22–3, 31–2
injuries, personal, 25, 46, 55, 58, 74–5, 81, 82, 170–2, 177–9
injuries, general, 78–83
learns to ride, 13
life as a jockey, 51–3, 87–101
marriage, 55
retires from racing, 209–10
school, 18–19, 24–6, 28
shows, 20–1, 26, 27–8
Smith's Hunting Stables, 17–21, 31, 34
techniques, 143–62
typical day of jockey, 102–12
walking the course, 51–2
war, 35–42
weather, 83–7
wins first race, 54
works and rides for George Owen, 48–61, 62–5
writing technique, 214

Francis, Douglas (author's brother), 13–16, 18–21, 22–4, 45, 48, 56, 165,198

Francis, Felix (author's son), 219

Francis, Mary (author's wife), 43, 44, 55, 62, 73–9, 85–6, 91, 104, 170–3, 176–7, 179–81, 188, 191, 198–9, 210, 217

Francis, Merrick (author's son), 219

Francis, Molly (author's mother), 14, 16–17, 19, 20–2, 25–6, 28, 30–5, 42–3, 44, 47, 74

Francis, Vincent (author's father), 13, 16, 19, 21–2, 26, 27–35, 42, 44–5, 47–8, 62, 74, 198

Francis, Willie (author's grandfather), 29

Francis, Mrs Willie (author's grandmother), 29

Freebooter, 113–14, 136

Freeman, Arthur, 195, 207

Gallery, 85

Galloway Braes, 128

Gentle Moya, 196

Gifford, Josh, 159

Gilbert, John, 159

Glendenning, Raymond, 159, 204

Grand National Steeplechase, 11, 12, 66–72

Grantham, Tony, 168, 174

Grayston, Jack, 18

Halloween, 113, 120

Happy Home, 116

Harries, Robert, 29

Hereford, 72

Hobbs, Bruce, 119–20

Hobbs, Reg, 66

Hurst Park course, 127–8

Inch Arran, 207

In View, 188

Islington Royal Agricultural Show, 27

Kempton Park course, 133–4

Kerstin, 192

Kirkland, 30

Levy Board Accident Scheme, 83

Lingfield course, 137, 138

Lochroe, 138, 170, 177, 190

Lort Phillips, Col, 30

Manicou, 175

Margaret, Princess, 20, 174, 195

Mariner's Log, 156, 168–71

Marshall, Bryan, 159, 174, 176, 178, 191

Marshall, Mary, 178

M'as-Tu-Vu, 173–5, 195–6, 204

Mason, Tich, 30

Mellor, Stan, 159

Milburn, George, 159

Mildmay, Lord, 66, 101, 129–30, 168–9

Mills, Bertram, 26–7

Moloney, Jack, 53

Molony, Martin, 62, 68–9, 81, 113, 114, 117, 159

Molony, Tim, 81, 97, 114, 116–17, 151, 159

Monaveen, 174, 175

Mont Tremblant, 113, 120, 190

Moseley, Mickey, 54

Murless, Noel, 207

Murphy, Joe, 53

McMorrow, Leo, 71

National Hunt Committee, 58, 163, 188

Newbury course, 135, 136

Noble Star, 120

O'Neil, Bobby, 50, 64

Ontray, 196

Oughton, Alan, 159

Owen, George, 48–55, 57, 58–65, 67, 71–2, 81, 88–9, 169

Owen, Margot, 48

Paget, Miss Dorothy, 120, 188
Paget, E. C., 169
Parthenon, 66, 68–9
Plumpton course, 136, 138–9, 142
Pondapatarri, 177
Power, Jimmy, 114
Prince of Denmark, 188

Quare Times, 96
Quick One, 88

Rank, J. V., 32
Red April, 116
Rees, Bill, 159
Rich, Herbert, 30–1
Richmond Horse Show, 21, 28
Rimell, Fred, 81, 151
Roimond, 65, 66, 68–70, 72, 77, 113, 115–18
Rompworthy, 55–6, 109
Rose Park, 175–7, 188, 207
Rowallan, Lord, 101
Royal Approach, 141
Russian Hero, 51–4, 57, 64, 70–2, 109, 116, 136

Salmon Renown, 57–8
Sandiacre, 206
Sandown Park course, 139–40, 142, 207
Scudamore, Michael, 159, 207
Selby, Bernard, 28
Senlac Hill, 156–7
Shahjem, 137
Sheila's Cottage, 136

Silver Fame, 64–6, 113–15, 117
Slack, George, 81, 159
Smith, Horace, 17, 18, 20
Smith's Hunting Stables, W. J., 17–18, 21, 31, 33–4
Smith's Riding School, Horace, 17
Southport Show, 26
Sprague, Harry, 159
Statecraft, 169
Sumner, Hugh, 213

Taaffe, Pat, 96, 141, 168
Thackeray, Fred, 81
Thelwell, Bob, 45
Thomas, Willie (author's grandfather), 14–15, 23–4
Thomas, Mrs Willie (author's grandmother), 15, 16, 23–4
Thompson, Arthur, 118
Tipperary Tim, 68
Towcester course, 138
Tucker, Bill, 75–6, 171, 178
Tulip, 25, 191

Vick, Lionel, 81

Wales, Prince of (later Duke of Windsor), 17
Walwyn, Fulke, 120
Weatherby & Co., 100
White, Hon. Mrs J., 168
Williams, Evan, 33
Williamson, Fearnie, 71, 72, 109
Winter, Fred, 80–1, 151, 160, 171, 193
Wootton, Stanley, 30
Wrenbury Tiger, 54, 220